And Now ...

Here's Max

MAX FERGUSON

On air: Max Ferguson (r) and Allan McFee

And Now ...

Here's Max

An Irreverent Memoir of the CBC by

MAX FERGUSON

With a new introduction by
Shelagh Rogers

SYBERTOOTH INC
SACKVILLE, NEW BRUNSWICK

Litteris Elegantis Madefimus

This edition published in 2009 by:

Sybertooth Inc.
59 Salem Street
Sackville, NB
E4L 4J6
Canada
www.sybertooth.ca

The paper is this edition is acid-free and meets all ANSI standards for archival
quality.

Library and Archives Canada Cataloguing in Publication

Ferguson, Max, 1924-
    And now -- here's Max / Max Ferguson ; with a foreword by Shelagh Rogers.

Originally published in 1967.
ISBN 978-0-9810244-7-9

    1. Ferguson, Max, 1924-. 2. Radio broadcasters--Canada--Biography.
3. Canadian Broadcasting Corporation--Biography. 4. Humorists, Canadian
(English)--20th century--Biography. 5. Radio broadcasting--Canada--Humour.
6. Canadian wit and humour (English). I. Title.

PN1991.4.F4A3 2009   791.44092   C2009-906170-8

INTRODUCTION

IN AN ARCHIVAL tape of an introduction to Max Ferguson, an announcer intones, "This is the story of how a handsome young Canadian man of education and character found himself as a nasty, hardbitten, dishonest, sarcastic, disreputable old man. A man of Max Ferguson's intelligence might have been anything. Perhaps even Prime Minister! But such was fate that he found himself and finds himself today as a whole stock company of voices doing sketches on the radio." He was bitten by the radio bug at university and never found the antidote to that bite. And thousands of Canadians are thankful.

There have been many mysteries at the CBC ... why they moved *The National* to 9pm, why they cancelled *The Friendly Giant*, why they tried to fire Max Ferguson (see pp. 116-117). Another is how it was that I was invited to become Max Ferguson's "sidekick" after the legendary Allan McFee (once perfectly described as the world's oldest "enfant terrible") retired. I didn't really know Max at the time. Sure, I'd seen him in the hallways of the Jarvis Street studios in downtown Toronto when he'd come in from his homes in the country to record his program. If it were summer, he'd be wearing his blue and white striped rugby shirt with some very short shorts. One couldn't help but notice, he was very fit. "Ripped" is how they would put it now. Before his recording time began, he usually roamed the building dropping off boxes of eggs from his own chickens to a number of fortunate producers. Whenever I saw him, I was very respectful, having grown up with Max's skewering political satire on the radio. I don't recall many words having passed between us. But perhaps it doesn't matter how it came to be. Some have greatness...in my case, working with Max ... thrust upon them. And I loved every minute.

I come from the post-*Rawhide* era of Max's time at the CBC. Once a week, for almost a decade, I sat across from him when he hosted his eponymous music show with the familiar Clarinet Polka as the opening theme. The music would fade down and we would just talk. After a few months, however, we were taken to task for our so-called "banal chit-chat". Topics were then provided for us as to talk about such as on this day in history beer was discovered, or King George went mad...and we were expected to riff for a couple of minutes on those topics. It didn't work. It turned out that listeners wanted conversation and they wrote in and asked why we were no longer talking about gardening, Newfoundland dogs, tales of Cape Breton winters and so on. A compromise was reached when we promised to keep the chit-chat to a two or three minute limit.

It was through these conversations that Max created one of his last characters. He made me into a dog-loving, periodically booze-swilling, sometimes slot-machine addicted, motorcycle Mama. Or, alternatively, The Wife of Bath. It was fine with me. For years, I had so often been cast as "the Mary Sunshine of CBC Radio" or "the girl with the smile in her voice". Max drew out another side: earthier perhaps, and definitely more natural. Whatever it was, it was heightened by Max's presence. There seemed to be more oxygen in the studio when he was there. And often, more nitrous oxide — laughing gas — as he would ask for instance, in all earnestness, about whether my dogs were neutered. I'd say yes. And he would tell me about implants which would allow my dog to still feel like one of the boys. Yes, he made me laugh — often to the point of weeping. I revelled in whatever he had to say and also in the way he said it.

Max loves the English language and proper usage. He despaired of how standards were slipping in that regard. He couldn't bear to hear nouns used as verbs as in "How did it impact his life?" (He would say it sounded like dental work) or adjectives derived from nouns as in the now ubiquitous "quality time". When announcers left out the first 'r' in February, he would cringe. He scoffed at euphemisms for change at the CBC such as "Creative Renewal" which almost always meant doing more with much less. We would receive memos in CBC-ese, being more planful (ouch) to be more impactful (yow). Max stood for clarity, precision and respect for the beauty of words used well, as you will see in the pages ahead.

When Max really and truly retired from the CBC in September of 1998, after 52 years of radio, I was hosting a classical music request program called *Take Five*. The day before his last broadcast, I read letters and played requests all dedicated to Max. I would have had him in the studio with me, but I knew his toes would have curled when he heard all the genuinely loving tributes that poured in...by the hundreds. From as far away as California, a fax came in which read: Dear Max, Thanks for everything. It was a great performance. Sincerely, Leonard (Leonard Cohen). From River Bourgeois on his beloved Cape Breton Island, Farley Mowat wrote that he had it on good authority that Rawhide was not a creation of Max Ferguson. It was the other way around. Tributes came in from Shanty Bay, Ontario, Gabriola Island BC, St. Lambert, Quebec, Winnipeg, Victoria, Saint John, and St. John's and Victoria and everywhere in between. The letters and emails talked about his wit and humour, his passion and commitment, his knowledge and his creativity. They loved his voice. Hear, hear. They called him unique, original, a renegade and even a reprobate (I really liked that one) and absolutely irreplaceable. And that has proven true. All of the tributes had this in common: Max Ferguson was part of their lives. They made a commitment to him, never missing his broadcasts. He was their friend.

There are several ways to define the word Max. One meaning is: the greatest possible quantity or degree. Another is: an upper limit permitted by law or other authority (see p. 62). But my favourites come from astronomy: the moment when a variable star is most brilliant...or the magnitude of the star at such a moment. They seem to suit the genius of Max Ferguson, though he would hate to think of himself as a "star". In a business of egos, he was and is, without a trace of ego. Max had many, many moments of brilliance. I witnessed some of them right across the table, as he connected so effortlessly with the audience. How did I get to be that witness every Saturday morning for almost ten years? Well, I got lucky — a phrase Max would have a field day with. I wouldn't have missed it for the world.

If this is your first time reading *And Now ... Here's Max*, I envy your maiden voyage. If it's your second or your fifth, well, you're part of a special club of revellers. Here's to Max — in all his glory. In the words he used to sign so many of his handwritten letters to listeners: May fortune smile.

Shelagh Rogers
September, 2009

I

WITH GREAT GROANS, creaks, and other forms of mechanical protest, the ancient elevator that grudgingly serviced the three floors of the old Free Press Building in London, Ontario, groped its way slowly down the shaft. I stood on the ground floor, peering up through the steel gate as the floor of the cage inched towards me. At about one second to touchdown, I thrust two fingers into my mouth and sent a piercing whistle reverberating up the shaft. This was a signal for Doug Trowell, waiting up on the third floor, to press his button and start the elevator back on its return trip. In due course, his whistle would come echoing down the shaft, and I would press my button to bring the poor, labouring beast back again. The game was called "Elevator", and the ritual had been going on for about ten minutes. Usually when we played Elevator, we released our captive passenger after two or three minutes, but this one, whoever he was, was giving us no satisfaction whatever. We must have sent him on at least fifty incarcerated round trips, and there hadn't been a sound from the cage. Normally at such times, the shaft would be an exhilarating cacophony of kicks, curses, pleadings, and poundings, but with a stoic spoilsport in the cage I was beginning to tire of the game and decided to let him out on his next trip down.

It was the summer of 1946. A month previously, and within a day or two of each other, Doug Trowell and I had joined the staff of radio station CFPL in London, Ontario. In a few short years, Doug would become manager of the station, and I would find myself in Halifax portraying a character called Rawhide on the CBC. But on this particular July afternoon in the old Free Press Building on Richmond Street, we were two very green 21-year-olds holding down our first regular jobs with one brief month of radio under our belts. Doug was earning twenty dollars a week and I, since I had my BA in English and French, was earning twenty-five — my first encounter with discrimination, although educationists would perhaps construe my additional five as a moral for would-be dropouts. In all fairness to the station management, I should point out that the services we rendered were certainly commensurate with our earnings. When we weren't playing Elevator, our main task was to put away piles of 78 rpm recordings left over from old radio programs — classical in one section, pops in another, children's records in another. It was in this challenging occupation that I came to realize the full value of my four-year background in French. From time to time we would encounter records with French titles, such as *L'Apres-Midi d'une Faune*. Whenever Doug carelessly filed this in the classical section, I was careful not to criticize but would tactfully and surreptitiously remove it later and slip it in beside *Bambi* in the children's section. It prevented chaos, of course, in the record library, but I still don't feel it warranted that extra five a week.

We had only been at CFPL about a week when we discovered in the station's antiquated elevator an unusual idiosyncrasy that I've never encountered in any other elevator. Whereas all other elevators unswervingly deliver their passengers to any designated floor and disgorge them before responding to a call from another floor, this senile old brute could easily be distracted from its duty to its passengers. At the very moment of debarkation, a buzz from any other floor would send it scurrying off like a woman of easy virtue — eager to service a newly found customer before the old one was decently dismissed. The practical application of this discovery became what we called our Elevator Game and helped while away many a long hour for us that summer.

Doug usually chose the third, or radio, floor of the Free Press Building, while I stationed myself on the main floor, which housed the newspaper operation. Then we'd simply wait until some unwitting employee got on at the second floor and the game began. The fact that we were wasting our employer's money never seriously impinged on our consciences. In the first place, we had earlier worked out our weekly salary to an hourly rate and discovered that our elevator diversion, when pro-rated, was about equivalent to one of his 60-watt bulbs burning for half an hour. In the second place, we had never met our employer. We knew only that his name was Walter J. Blackburn and that he owned both the radio station and the newspaper. He was an awesome but impersonal being, having about as much reality in our lives as Victoria had in Gunga Din's. He had been pointed out to me once at a distance and identified in hushed tones — a tall, dark man with black, craggy eye-brows and flashing eyes who reminded me instantly of Rudolph Hess.

Now, as the elevator descended for what must have been the sixtieth time and wheezed to a stop in front of me, I wasn't a bit concerned that we had incarcerated one of Mr. Blackburn's employees, perhaps even a senior editor, for almost fifteen unproductive minutes. What did concern me was that the wretch inside the cage, with his Spartan sangfroid, had robbed us of a lot of fun. With a wobbly clank, both door and gate slid back together, and at last tormentor and tormented stood face to face. He was a tall, dark man with black, craggy eyebrows who reminded me instantly of ... Rudolph Hess! My stomach walls came together in a sort of acid-exuding embrace with the realization that our silent victim had, indeed, been Walter J. Blackburn.

Now, too late, I knew why he hadn't made a sound. He was saving it all for one terrifying, maniacal explosion, and the moment was at hand. His lips began working in an ashen face. Words were being formed but, as yet, there was no sound — just a small, throbbing paroxysm of suppressed fury working on one cheek. Had he suddenly shouted at me that Hitler really wanted to be friends with England I couldn't have been more surprised than I was when his speech finally returned. In a controlled and only slightly strangulated voice he said, "I don't want you to fool with this elevator again," and then walked off. That was all. Not another word. But during the rest of my stay at CFPL, we never again played the Elevator Game.

As the summer wore on, I was given more and more on-air broadcasting assignments and gradually began to achieve an identity. I was emerging from the unglamorous cocoon of joe-boy into the multi-hued, butterfly world of the radio announcer. But poor old Doug Trowell was still thrashing around inside his cocoon. Not a soul at CFPL that summer, least of all Doug himself, could figure out just what Doug was supposed to be doing there. Our station manager, Don Wright (later to brighten the CBC network with his excellent choral group) confided in me one day that when Doug had approached him for a job, he had had absolutely no opening for him. "But the guy was so darn funny," said Don, "that I hired him just to have him around."

There were many times that summer around the studios when Don Wright must have gagged on those words. Doug Trowell was funny, alright ... there was no denying that. I could enjoy more laughs in one minute from Doug Trowell than I could in a lifetime of Bob Hope, Red Skelton, and Danny Kaye combined. The only problem was that around CFPL that summer there was no legally authorized outlet for Doug's brilliant impromptu flights of comic invention. Consequently, when the mood was upon him, he had the habit of heading lemming-like for the nearest studio and, regardless of what program was in progress, he would burst in upon the poor devils trying to do their job and utterly devastate them and the program.

One of his characterizations was an old salt whom he called Scott C. Mulsion. He got the idea from the label of those cod-liver oil bottles whose labels always carried the picture of a grizzled old chap in oilskins and a sou'wester, bent double under the weight of a huge codfish which he had slung over his back. I can well remember standing around the microphone with three other actors in Studio B, partway through a dramatic sketch, when the door of the studio flew open and in came Doug Trowell, a battered fedora on his head with the brim pulled down all the way 'round to suggest a sou'wester. His hands gripped an imaginary fish-line, and he was bent double under the weight of a huge, nonexistent cod slung over his back. To make matters worse, whenever he was Scott C. Mulsion, Doug always spoke in that crazy, sub-human voice which I later blatantly stole and used for the loudmouthed character on my Rawhide program. He fixed us with a wild stare for several agonizing seconds, while we desperately tried to ignore him and carry on in the character roles we were portraying.

Then came that awful voice. "I'se Scott C. Mulsion. Man and boy, dere, I'se carried dis here codfish on me back for over forty years, and I'se worth ten of any of youse, dere. What are yez all doin' dere sayin' all dem crazy things into dat microphone? What are yez talkin' in dem crazy voices for? What's wrong wid your real voices? I know all of yez, and I'm sick of your tomfoolery. Yes, I mean you, Roy Kervin and Max Ferguson, and Keith Chase!"

At this point, while we tried vainly to hold onto our character voices in the play, good old Scott C. Mulsion named every one of us by our real names, the ones by which we were pretty well known around London. For actors even of our humble status, this was something akin to being stripped naked at the corner of Bloor and Yonge. He then staggered to the studio door, turned to emit three raucous but incredibly realistic seagull cries, and vanished, leaving us in the ruins of our play, hopelessly trying to win back the listeners' "willing suspension of disbelief".

CFPL's most prestigious program that summer was a nine o'clock morning newscast sponsored by the London branch of one of Canada's foremost department store chains. This dandy little money earner was held in such high esteem by management that it was never entrusted to just one announcer. It was always a two-man job. CFPL's chief announcer, John Trethewey (now with the CBC's Montreal outlet) handled the principal duties, and my first "big-time" break came when I was appointed second announcer. In this role, sharp on the dot of nine each morning, I would shout into the microphone in an embryo Marvin Mellobell voice, "Headlines of Your World Today!!!"

Then, seated next to me at his microphone, John

Trethewey, in a much more mature and authoritative voice, would read out three dramatic world headlines.

While he rested from the effort, I leaped in again with, "In a moment, the details of these stories, but first —" At this juncture, London matrons enjoying their second cup of coffee by their radios would learn what delights awaited them that morning at our sponsor's store in the way of panties, half slips, or nursing brassieres. After one minute the ladies and I would return from our jaunt to Nirvana, and Trethewey would continue on prosaically with the main body of the news. From all this you can certainly see that the Huntley-Brinkley idea is not a new one.

One morning in mid-August, the above-outline format had rolled on with all the smoothness of a Rolls engine, and Trethewey was just nearing the end of his news. With less than two minutes to go he launched into a news item that recalled that this very morning was the anniversary of the death of Jumbo, the gargantuan Barnum and Bailey elephant who had been killed many years before while crossing the railway tracks at St. Thomas, Ontario, about eighteen miles from London. John had just reached the line, "... and was carried off by an untimely death as he lumbered across the tracks at St. Thomas into the path of a through train in the year ...."

There was a momentary pause, a hesitance over the date.

I had been sitting rather inattentively up to this point, probably planning how much candy I'd be able to buy with my twenty-five dollars that week, when I suddenly realized that John's voice had ground to a halt. Shooting a quick glance across at the news copy that was lying on the table in front of him, I soon spotted the reason the cat had his tongue. In place of the date of Jumbo's death on the yellow news copy were two asterisks, a comma, and a capital N. Teletype machines have a habit of doing this whenever, due to atmospheric conditions, their clever little metal fingers became all thumbs. Since Trethewey was in the habit of visiting the teletype machines at about two minutes to air time and ripping off huge fistfuls of news, he hadn't been able to read it over carefully and foresee this trap he'd now fallen into. However, to his credit, he was nonplussed for only a second or two. Even back in those days he'd been in the business long enough to have learned the announcers' credo, "Fake it and force on!" Completely at random, he pulled the date, 1900, out of the air, and confident that no-one had noticed his momentary dilemma, continued smoothly on.

To this day I don't know how Doug Trowell reacted so quickly. Of course, he was always lurking outside studio doors, waiting hopefully. I think he must have had an antici-patory sixth sense that could spot moments of on-air distress even before they occurred. Whenever he felt that tiny tele-pathic tug on the finely spun silk of his maliciously invent-ive mind, he never failed to pounce. At any rate, there he was within three seconds of Trethewey's hesitation over the date of Jumbo's death, lumbering through the studio door. He had removed his suit coat and thrown it over his head, so that one empty sleeve hung down in front and was swinging to and fro like an elephant's trunk. He stopped a foot or two inside the studio and emitted one or two muffled stentorian grunts from underneath the coat. Fortunately Trethewey hadn't seen or heard him yet, and I was far enough to one side that my con-vulsive heavings of desperately stifled laughter weren't vis-ible to the golden voice of our biggest commercial account. I clung to the hope that Trowell, satisfied with the reaction he was getting from me, would now abandon his little charade and withdraw. Trowell, however, was just warming up.

He began to lumber slowly around the studio, the empty sleeve swinging back and forth in front of him, until he came up immediately behind Trethewey, who was still rolling on with all the confidence in the world, telling listeners how big a void had been left in the hearts of all who had seen and loved old Jumbo. Trethewey never really had a chance. His first in-timation of impending disaster was when Jumbo's clumsily reincarnated trunk slithered obscenely over his face from behind. When the open end of the empty sleeve was directly in front of the microphone, a hollow, booming voice rolled out with the indignant correction, "I was killed in 1885!"

I have never since seen a break-up in radio to equal that

one. The operator behind the control-room glass was too dumbfounded to even cut the mikes and fill with recorded music. Trethewey and I made no attempt to stifle our explosion of laughter. To have done so would have meant a double hernia for both of us. We simply folded our arms on the table in front of us, and resting our heads on our arms so that our respective mouths each faced an open mike, we laughed, hysterically and uncontrollably, for the remaining ninety seconds of sponsored time. For all the rest of that day, CFPL management conferred behind closed doors with outraged executives of the big department store. Rumours flew that our nine o'clock gold mine was finished, but eventually the dark clouds blew over and there was peace in our time.

When it came to nurturing the spiritual growth of its listeners, CFPL was certainly no slouch. I'm sure one of the most unique, if not bizarre, religious programs to be aired over any station in Canada was a once-a-week evening spectacular called *The Gospel Ship*. A small knot of five or six men and women whom nobody seemed to know and who, I always felt, simply wandered in off Richmond Street to escape either rain or noisy traffic used to take their places in Studio B. When the on-air light flashed, one of their number, a meek little man, stepped up to the microphone with a hot-water bottle and began sloshing the contents back and forth for about twenty seconds. Then in a most plaintive, almost whining voice (I'm still using it as one of my radio character voices) he would ask, "Won't you come aboard the Gospel Ship, where you're never a stranger twice?"

From the program's inception, Doug Trowell and I would never miss one of these openings. Somehow our hearts went out to this poignant little fellow as we stood watching that strange opening each week with our faces pressed against the studio window. To us he was a symbol of courage against odds, a synthesis of all the world's lost causes, turning up week after week with his hot-water bottle, gamely attempting, through the magic of radio, to evoke in the listeners' minds that wonderful world of make-believe — striving to make them see and feel the sting of salt spray as white-foamed

16

breakers hurled themselves against the shuddering hull of the Gospel Ship. And all the while there wasn't a hope in hell of the listeners' seeing anything in their mind's eye except someone standing in front of a microphone, sloshing water back and forth in a hot-water bottle.

Of quite a different order was CFPL's weekday morning religious program, *In the Chapel.* This calm, tranquil program was to be the vehicle through which Doug Trowell earned for himself a special niche in the Radio Hall of Infamy and in the process put me through the most petrifying experience of my radio career to date. *In the Chapel* opened each morning at 8:30 with the playing of sacred choral music on record. At the end of the first verse, the operator in the control room would fade down the recording and open my microphone. Then in my most sanctimonious voice I would read from a prepared script, "As the doors of the chapel open and the swelling voices of the choir are heard, won't you join us for a few quiet moments ... (dramatic pause) ... In the Chapel?" At this point I would introduce the morning's guest minister, who would fill the rest of the fifteen minutes with a prepared sermon and a final blessing. Then over a soft background of sacred music I would sign the program off with the mellifluous invitation to, "Join us again tomorrow for a few quiet moments ... In the Chapel."

On the Doomsday morning in question, the control room operator informed me at about two minutes to air time that we would have no guest minister that morning. He hadn't shown up. After a hurried consultation, it was agreed that I would make an apology announcement and the operator would fill the time with sacred recordings. We got the program underway and I was in the middle of explaining, with divinely inspired ad-lib, that our guest minister was unable to be with us In the Chapel on this occasion. Suddenly my words were interrupted by the noisy opening of the studio door. I glanced up briefly and saw what I thought was our missing minister — black vestment all across the front with a flash of white collar just showing above. The figure had his hand extended toward me in what seemed at the moment to be a natural and characteristic gesture of Christian fellowship and goodwill. I was halfway out of my chair to accept the extended hand, when suddenly it dawned on me — it was Doug Trowell! He had removed his tie and was wearing his suit coat back to front. The face was wreathed from ear to ear in a warm Christian smile.

Determined not to give him the slightest encouragement, I sank back in my chair and continued on with my interrupted apology announcement. I could feel the saliva begin to dry in my mouth as I watched him noisily settling himself into the empty minister's chair beside me, obviously, getting ready to say something. I shot an anguished glance at the on-air light on the studio wall, desperately hoping to find it off. But there it was, burning brightly, and indicating that the operator had not killed the studio microphones. I couldn't even give a "cut" signal, because there wasn't a sign of the operator through the control-room window.

"Well, Mr. Ferguson," Trowell began with a hearty slap on my shoulder, "this is certainly one hell of a way to arrive for a broadcast. Believe me, I ran like a son of a bitch all the way from my church, but you know what that bloody traffic's like on Richmond Street. I sure as hell hope I haven't ruined the damn program."

At this point he had not only ruined the program, the series, and both our jobs, but had partially destroyed, I was certain, about four square feet of my acid-corroded stomach lining. I longed to be able to tell him all this, but with the mikes open I could do no more than fix him with a look of panic-stricken appeal, which he blithely ignored. Before the fifteen-minute ordeal had ended, he managed to fit in an off-colour sermon and two or three smutty parables, all delivered in a very prim and proper ministerial voice.

I seemed to sound horribly implicated in the whole disaster when I signed off in thin, quavering tones, "Won't you join us again tomorrow for a few quiet moments ... In the Chapel?" I don't really know why I bothered. It was a pretty safe bet that nobody would be joining me tomorrow, next week, next year, or ever again in the shattered ruins of that little chapel. Trowell let me languish in a blue funk all that day before divulging that the whole thing had been rigged for my benefit. With the operator's electronic connivance, the on-air light was kept burning, even though the studio mikes had been safely cut (a trick I've never seen done since), and while the listening audience were fed a program of recorded sacred music from the control room, my ears and my ears alone were assailed by Trowell's nightmarish performance.

In these past few pages I may have given the wrong impression of Doug Trowell. He wasn't altogether destructive. All he really needed was a legally authorized outlet for his considerable talent, energy, and wild imagination. This eventually came about as we moved into the early autumn of 1946 and our station manager, Don Wright, offered Doug and me the chance to tackle in our own fashion a daily half-hour program in the late afternoon. We used to play records interspersed with ad-lib skits, and though we enjoyed it immensely and used to break each other up every ten seconds, there was not, throughout the entire run of the program, one single letter or phone call. Undaunted, Doug went out one day and lined up a sponsor — a nursery just outside the city limits called the London Little Tree Farm.

We were absolutely elated, walking on air like a couple of latter-day Dick Whittingtons who had suddenly discovered that the streets of *their* London were also paved with gold. We decided to make the Little Tree Farm commercials a bit more palatable by camouflaging them within the framework of a skit, which we would ad-lib on each program. On the first momentous day of our newly achieved commercial status it was decided that I would play the role of an average London citizen going out to buy a tree and Doug would portray the manager of the Little Tree Farm. Somewhere among the meagre pickings of CFPL's sound library we managed to dig up a recording of chirping birds, and with this background we plunged hopefully into that all-important first commercial.

My opening line was the brilliantly conceived, "Hello, there, I'd like to buy one of your trees."

Then Doug flashed back with, "Oh?"

For a moment I was a bit disconcerted to hear the manager of the tree farm — our sponsor — portrayed by Doug in his horrible, unearthly Scott C. Mulsion voice, but I pushed on, and the little sketch began to develop beautifully. We were managing to get across all the essential selling points of the commercial and at the same time were keeping things light and humorous. We'd been going for about four minutes when I decided to toss Doug a cue line to round out the skit like the double beat of the bass drum in a military band.

"Well," I began, in the voice of a well-satisfied customer, "You've certainly sold me on the London Little Tree Farm. I'll take that young spruce over there."

Now all Doug had to say was, "Fine," or "Thank you," or, "Come back again," and we'd have been home free. Instead he chose to round off with, "Yessir, boy, you'll never regret it. You'll soon discover, like thousands of other satisfied customers, that when it come to our trees — their bark is worse than their blight!"

The next day we learned that the Little Tree Farm had decided, in spite of all the risks and vicissitudes, to plunge on into the competitive world of business without a helping hand from us.

Within two weeks of the tree farm's reckless decision to go it alone, I received a letter from the CBC asking would I like to become part of the big happy family by joining the Halifax station as a staff announcer. Even before coming to CFPL at the beginning of the summer, I had auditioned for the CBC in Toronto and had been told to first of all gain some experience with a private station. Thanks largely to Doug Trowell, my brief summer at CFPL made me feel more than ready to cope with any challenge network radio might offer, so I accepted the invitation and arrived in Halifax, a living, breathing, flesh-and-blood CBC announcer on December 6, 1946.

II

LIKE A FURIOUS and savage watchdog hurling itself at an intruder, the wind whipped down off Citadel Hill to challenge me as I fought my way up South Park Street on a forty-five degree slant. I was heading for the CBC Halifax studios, and my first evening of duty as a CBC announcer. The elevator in the United Service Building, which housed the CBC, disgorged me at the third floor, and I stepped out to face a double-glassed door that bore the awesome lettering, CANADIAN BROADCASTING CORPORATION. Below the lettering was the blue and red CBC crest, giving one the impression that he was entering the ancestral estate of a very old and very staid British dynastic family. I thought, as I slowly pushed on the big brass handle, of all the epithets I had heard applied to this venerable dowager by the private station people from whom I'd come — autocratic, stuffy, terribly formal — and for a moment I was engulfed by a wave of nostalgia for the carefree, uninhibited, and very easygoing life at CFPL. Then the door opened and I took my first step into the world of national radio.

For the next twenty minutes that first step was to be as far as I was going to get into the world of national radio. My path was blocked by about two dozen wildly yelling, whooping, laughing bodies — the staff of the CBC Halifax station. Without a word of greeting or explanation, a stiff belt of Maritime rum was thrust at me by an unsteady hand, and I felt myself swept up in a noisy, obstreperous, mammoth charade. Considering the date, December 7, the subject could well have been the Japanese attack on Pearl Harbour. In reality it turned out merely to be an impromptu going-away thrash for a very popular CBC Halifax technical type who was parting company with his corporate employer at the latter's request. The unfortunate choice of a fully loaded silver flask as a going-away present had apparently triggered the bacchanal. To make matters worse, each time they said goodbye to the "birthday boy" and sent him out the door with cries of, "God bless you!" "All the best!" "Don't forget to write!", he would get only as far as the street door. Then the icy blast of a Halifax December night would send him lurching back up to the third floor CBC offices to repeat the maudlin scene all over again. This had been going on since four o'clock in the afternoon. Careful not to antagonize any of my newly found CBC cousins, I downed the last of my raw rum and reached the safety and quiet of little studio C, which was to be my home for the rest of the evening. It was a bit of a shock to hear my first network cue, the deep, resonant one I'd been polishing up for days, finally dribbling out of a rum-scorched mouth like a load of wet cement.

Like any new announcer at any radio station, I fell heir to the unpopular night shift, which began at six p.m. and ended with the station sign-off a few minutes after midnight. There was very little to do, of course, except insert a local station call every thirty minutes or so. I used to sit by the hour in master control, sharing the monotony of the long evening with the engineer on duty. Occasionally an unexpected visitor might drop in. This happened one evening during my third or fourth night on duty for the Corporation, when the chief announcer, Syd Kennedy, burst into master control, flung an old-fashioned wire recorder into the corner in disgust, and spent the next five minutes pacing up and down, purging his nervous system of some vast, annoying frustration by means of an emotional catharsis which must have employed every swear word known to the English-speaking world. This puzzled me, since I'd seen him leave a few hours earlier on what appeared to be a very simple and pleasant assignment. He was off to HMCS *Stadacona* to record highlights of the annual Christmas concert held for dependents of naval personnel on the base, and he was in high good humour. When the fumings and splutterings had finally settled down into understandable English, he unfolded his problems to us, and thereby hangs one of the most bizarre Santa Claus stories I've ever heard.

Kennedy had wanted to get enough recorded material at the *Stadacona* Christmas concert to put together a fifteen-minute human interest program for broadcast the next day. Realizing that old Santa's arrival and the resultant cheers and squeals of delight from the children would be the focal point of interest in any such endeavour, he had gone backstage with his wire recorder and was waiting in the wings of the base auditorium to be sure to catch the jolly old fellow the moment he came in. The jolly old fellow came in, alright, but with several naval types supporting him. They sat him on a chair — a big, roly-poly, able-bodied seaman stoned to the eyeballs — and while some slapped his flaccid face and threw water on it, others struggled to insert the limp legs into red flannel breeches and stuff the dangling arms into the sleeves of the jolly red jacket.

Finally they got him up onto his feet, straightened the beard, and slung the sack of goodies over his shoulder. He marched manfully out onto the stage, made a fairly presentable left wheel, and stood facing the joyful bedlam of delight which burst forth from hundreds of ecstatic little voices. All he had to do was stand there and wave, and none would have been the wiser. But this wasn't playing the game with Nelson and his dying exhortation to men of the sea. Duty demanded a good, rousing, "Oh, ho, ho!" and in spite of his condition he decided to give it a try. The deep-seated muscular effort required to produce such a sound proved to be the last straw for an already turbulent stomach. Along with the "Oh, ho, ho!" it offered up its entire contents in one immense, volatile trajectory that extended out over the footlights and was immediately followed by the loveable old gentleman himself, who pitched forward on his face and lay in a shocking heap while hundreds of confused and frightened children turned up tear-streaked faces to their parents, waiting for some comforting words of explanation that just didn't come.

Sometimes as I sat whiling away the evening hours in master control, the various technical engineers on duty would try to drum into my head a modest rudimentary knowledge of the technical side of radio. There was a large metal cabinet which caught my fancy one evening; through the grill I could see various lights and what looked like pretty-coloured, beaded necklaces. This, they told me, was the CBC Halifax transmitter, which sent the voice of the CBC out over the city of Halifax with a mighty surge of 100 watts and carried it right to the city limits.

They spent many a patient hour trying to teach me which were the filaments and which were the plates. They had impressive names for every one of the myriad tubes that made up the electronic guts of the transmitter, an exotic nomenclature that included gems such as "audio oscillator tube". To their ultimate disgust, I ended up with my own system of designation. All the tubes in the top half of the transmitter were Eustachian, and all those in the bottom were fallopian. In moments of crisis when the transmitter broke down, with bodies racing to and fro and tension mounting, I couldn't resist elbowing my way into the semi-circle of perplexed engineers who stood around the ailing transmitter like so many doctors trying to diagnose a patient. There was a certain feeling of importance, a sense of belonging to a team, and though it brought me nothing but scowls, I always tried to help out with suggestions, such as, "That's a pretty inflamed Eustachian tube, if you ask me," or, "It looks to me as if there might be an egg stuck in that fallopian tube."

This latter suggestion wasn't quite as inane as it appeared on the surface. Beneath its farcical exterior lay a certain irony that they would never dream of. In the absence of eggs I used to stick a large, greasy load of fish and chips into those same tubes almost every evening. Those were my bachelor days in Halifax, and since I was saving every penny I earned in the hope of buying a sailboat, I used to eat rather frugally. For the first few weeks I always brought along on the night shift a tin of Irish stew, which I would place on a little hot-plate in the newsroom immediately upon arriving at six p.m. Then around seven o'clock, when it was nicely warmed, I would remove the tin from the hotplate and consume the contents. One evening, however, I completely forgot about the tin until almost ten p.m. I raced for the newsroom door and had just stepped

24

over the threshold when one of the most deafening explosions I've ever heard suddenly went off. In all seriousness I was convinced another munitions ship had gone up in Halifax harbour. In a moment or two I connected the explosion with the tin of Irish stew and stepped into the teletype room to find all four walls dripping with steaming lumps of potato and meat. The gravy had drenched all the teletype machines, yet the little keys were valiantly pounding out their soggy staccato of news. I was there until one in the morning mopping up the mess so the morning newsroom crew wouldn't see it. This incident finished me with Irish stew, and from then on I allowed myself the extravagance of ordering fish and chips when I came on duty.

You had to be more than just hungry to tackle such greasy fare night after night; you had to be ravenous. And so I used to wait until about nine o'clock for my appetite to reach such a state of desperation. The question was how to keep the food warm until that time. That's how I hit upon the idea of opening the transmitter door each evening when no one was looking and laying the entire mess down on the hot tubes, which made a perfect warming oven. There was no risk involved, because the engineers, as part of my ill-fated electronic instruction, had told me that the high voltage was cut off when the transmitter door was opened. This also meant that each evening, as I lovingly laid my greasy supper to rest on the tubes, the citizens of Halifax were deprived for approximately thirty seconds of their very own national broadcasting service.

Each evening, the master control engineer, before leaving the building after the station signed off, would type up the daily broadcast log, a faithful enumeration of every bit of program material that had gone out over the transmitter during the course of the broadcast day. He would then leave it on management's desk as his last ritual of the day. And each morning at nine, an exasperated management would glance down the log to find the same recurring entry, "Thirty second cut in program feed ex transmitter." In the two and a half years I was down there, the best CBC technical brains in the Maritimes puzzled over that one and never did come up with the answer.

The number-one man in the CBC's Maritime operation back in 1946 was Commander W.E.S. Briggs. Considering the CBC's predilection for full-blown Gilbert and Sullivan titles, his was fairly terse — Maritime Regional Representative. He'd come to the CBC straight from his first love, the Royal Canadian Navy, which he'd served with distinction; for this reason he was always referred to as "the old man". On my second day on the job I was informed that the old man would like to see me in his office for the customary indoctrination talk given all new employees. Fortunately, I knew what to expect. Briggs had often been described to me, long before I'd even thought of going into radio, by two of my friends in London, Ontario, who'd served under him in the North Atlantic. I wonder, though, how many new CBC Halifax employees, summoned for the first time to meet the old man and not grasping the special naval significance of the term, expected to be ushered in by a benign, white-haired old gentleman who evoked memories of Dad, Santa, and the local minister. What a rude awakening they must have had! Briggs was built like a British bulldog and stood with the same solidity that a sumo wrestler squats. Even without his beard, which had only recently been removed either out of deference to or contempt of civilian life, he was still as fearsome-looking a character as you'd want to meet. *As* our meeting drew to a close, he fixed me across his desk with a pair of hard, glinting, grey eyes that wouldn't have blinked with a blowtorch on them and said, "You'll find, Ferguson, I always lay my cards on the table. In my region you can make any mistake in the book," (here the normally square jaw became oblong as it thrust forward a full inch) "but just make it once." In the three years I was to work under him in Halifax the only mistake I can clearly recall making twice was when I arrived late in studio C for the one o'clock Maritime news on two successive Christmas Eves. On both occasions I had been waylaid and detained by one W.E.S. Briggs who insisted I share a festive cup with him in honour of the season.

As a throwback to his navy days, Briggs made quite a

ceremony out of his weekly tours of inspection. Gathering up his various department heads into a little entourage, he would walk the length and breadth of the CBC offices and studios, ferreting out anything that smacked of an inefficient or "un-tiddley" ship. After the tour was completed, the reluctant acolytes would be herded into one of the partitioned offices, where Briggs would comment on his findings in a sort of State of the Corporation address. I can remember catching the tail end of one such summation as I sneaked past one day on the other side of the partition. "I'm not overly disturbed," Briggs was saying, "at finding dust all over the announcers' desks. And the disgusting sight of stale cigarettes floating in abandoned coffee cups in the newsroom can probably be forgotten in time, but ..." (here the deceptively muted strings gave way to a full brass crescendo), "by thundering —, if I ever again get — strawberry jam on my fingers when I open the door to studio C, there'll be proper hell to pay!" In a CBC region such as Halifax, where all announcers were issued with dusting cloths whenever a top executive was expected from CBC headquarters in Ottawa, the thought of Commander Briggs' jammy fingers was just too much. I let out an explosive guffaw on the other side of the partition and then, realizing that this would hardly pour oil on the troubled waters, I ran like the wind.

From all this I've probably given the impression that Briggs ran a tight ship. As he sat, until recently, in the CBC headquarters building in Ottawa, number two man in the Corporation, this certainly seemed to be one of the favourite taunts hurled at him in the press by his detractors. Whenever I read this accusation of the tight ship, I recalled those old Halifax days, the mornings just before nine when half the staff would gravitate to the tiny newsroom and sit about drinking mugs of hot coffee well laced with rum. I remember the staff baseball games on the common just in front of the CBC building at the base of Citadel Hill, and I can see Briggs clearly crowding home plate and holding the bat in a cricket stance. He used to lift the ball far enough for the average person to make it at least two dozen times around the bases, but not having been endowed with the build of a sprinter, Briggs always had a close call getting to third.

That tight ship even had enough esprit de corps to field a rather motley CBC hockey team in Halifax's industrial league. In the absence of money for proper equipment, one of our operators, whom we called Big Stanislaus, used to fashion the most grotesque athletic supports out of old acetate recordings softened over heat, moulded into shape, and then fastened on with adhesive tape. Before every game in the privacy of his living room, his solicitous wife would test the device by slashing him in the pubic area with a hockey stick. If he wasn't sick on the rug, he was pronounced ready for the fray.

I often recall, too, the many times we'd be chased — literally chased — through that tight ship by Briggs for some misdemeanour he'd discovered. At such times we'd always race for the newsroom. Invariably as Briggs attempted to follow us in over the threshold, one of the editors, Fred Brickenden, would plant his large Winnipeg frame squarely in the doorway and below at Briggs in a voice accustomed to making itself heard over vast windswept prairie expanses, "Hold and bloody well forbear! Wot ye not that this poor wretch hath now benefit of sanctuary? Out I say and tread ye not upon this sanctified ground!" Briggs would fume and make loud, mock protestations of mutiny and insubordination. Then he'd beat a retreat to his office next door while we carried off our end of the charade, cringing and peering through Brickenden's legs.

There was also the occasion aboard the tight ship when Briggs caught me leaving the announce booth during my shift of duty. Booth duty, always the bane of announcers' lives, was a boring and stultifying experience which required an announcer to sit through several hours of network programs from Vancouver, Winnipeg, Toronto, and Montreal. At the end of each fifteen-minute or half-hour program, the Halifax booth announcer would have to be on the spot to come in and identify the local station with the call letters, CBH. Briggs, two days previous to this particular incident, had reaffirmed in a memo to all announcers that they were to stick to their post and avoid missing station calls. It was a Saturday afternoon and I'd been on booth duty for about four hours in the little Black Hole of Calcutta that we called Studio C. Longing for the sound of a human voice, I opened the studio door and started heading down the long studio corridor that led to the outer offices. I had only gone a few steps when I saw the door at the far end of the corridor suddenly open, and there was Briggs, advancing like a dreadnought straight for me. I immediately beat a guilty retreat back to the studio and closed the door. My eyes were fixed on the tiny peephole window that is standard equipment on all CBC studio doors. Sure enough, in a matter of moments a large, disembodied, cyclopic eye appeared at the little window, glared at me accusingly for a few seconds, then vanished.

At the time, Toronto was feeding us down the network a half-hour serialized dramatization of *The Count of Monte Cristo*. When I heard the last of Briggs' footsteps retreating down the corridor, I was seized with a sudden impulse to jump up and enact, solely for the benefit of the bored operator on the other side of the control-room glass, my own version of Monte Cristo. I pounded with clenched fists on the studio door, yelling in full-blown Barrymore style, "Let me out! In God's name, let me out! Must I be shut up here forever? Must I never see the sky again?" and so on. After about a minute of this I sat down again. Soon there was a small clicking noise behind me, and I turned in time to see the studio door opening very slowly. It opened just wide enough for a hand to come through, a hand that dropped a small, stale crust of bread on the studio floor and then withdrew. While I sat staring down at the crust, wondering which of the several engineering nuts on duty that afternoon had responded so appropriately to my charade, the operator, whose view faced the corridor, put down his talk-back switch and said, "That Uncle Bulgy's a character, eh?" Uncle Bulgy was the secretly whispered code name among the Halifax staff for Commander W.E.S. Briggs.

I've been deliberating whether or not to pass along my favourite item of Briggsiana. It comes uncomfortably close to telling tales out of school, but I think enough time has passed and enough water gone under the bridge that none of the parties involved will be too grieved by its disclosure. Briggs always had, and still has, a great fondness and respect for outside or remote broadcasting. The technique is probably the most demanding in radio or TV and calls for a broadcaster to not only think on his feet, but also to have sufficient imagination and vocabulary to make any scene come alive for the listening audience in the most fresh, original, and arresting way possible. I have yet to hear anyone in North American radio who can touch Briggs in this area. In that vast, barren desert of stilted speech, hushed tones, and outright sycophancy which engulfed every Royal Tour broadcast the CBC attempted, Briggs' voice bubbled through always like a refreshing brook. Unlike so many of his fellow observers, he never seemed to confuse the occasion with the Second Coming.

As would be expected then, we did a lot of outside broadcasting in the Halifax region. If Briggs wasn't actually taking part, he generally came along to observe. Sometimes, as in the case of the Wedgeport International Tuna Tournament or the Annapolis Valley Apple-blossom Festival, we'd be on the scene for three or four days. On these occasions, far removed from the studios and the need to maintain a reasonably decorous behaviour, Briggs was an absolute fiend for practical jokes. One spring evening in the late forties, a CBC Halifax outside broadcast crew returned to their rooms at the charming, sequestered old Cornwallis Inn at Kentville in the Annapolis Valley. Syd Kennedy, the Halifax station manager and producer of the outside broadcast they'd been working on all day, was utterly exhausted, but there was to be little sleep waiting from him that night. As usual Briggs would keep everyone up till about four in the morning, shooting the breeze and splicing the main-brace. When Syd finally escaped and dragged his weary feet back to his own room, he flung his exhausted body onto the hotel-room bed. The whole thing then came down around his ears with a resounding crash, understandably weakened by Briggs' having sawn through all four legs.

The rest of the crew, who for the past few days had

experienced an endless round of similar indignities, were more than willing when Syd invited them to participate in a vengeful conspiracy he'd hatched for the following evening. When zero hour arrived that next night, they all sauntered innocently into Briggs' room. He, at the moment, was in the bathroom taking his accustomed shower. They faked a loud knocking on the hotel-room door, and one of the group yelled in to Briggs that he was wanted at the door.

Wrapping a bath towel around his middle and still dripping wet, Briggs advanced to the door like a mobile segment of Stonehenge. The second he opened the door, several pairs of eager hands shoved him out into the hall, while still more eager hands pulled the bath towel the opposite way — back into the room. Body and towel parted company on either side of a hastily locked door. Briggs began to pound as loudly as he dared without arousing a hall-full of guests. Alternate appeals and threats were hissed through the keyhole, but Briggs' nightmare was only beginning. Just as the Russian peasants, when they finally turned on the Czar in 1917, didn't stop at the palace gates, so this handful of long-suffering victims decided to make the most of their golden moment. The manager of the inn was phoned and the complaint lodged that a nude man was annoying them by pounding on their hotel-room door and trying to force entry. The upshot of the whole business was that the CBC was banned for several years from the Cornwallis Inn.

The one remote or outside broadcast that stands out most memorably in my mind was the International Tuna Tournament. This event is held annually at Wedgeport, a fishing village on the extreme western tip of the Nova Scotia peninsula. The date is usually set for late August or early September to coincide with the arrival in Nova Scotian waters of the schools of giant tuna which have spent the summer steadily and leisurely migrating north from the Caribbean along the Atlantic seaboard. Teams from various parts of the world arrive in Wedgeport each year at this time to compete with one another in several categories: the greatest number of tuna caught in a single day, the greatest total weight of tuna caught in a single day, the largest single tuna caught in any one day, and of course, the largest tuna caught during the entire tournament.

The CBC has covered this event on network radio since its inception, and it was my good fortune to get in on one of the early broadcasts back in September of 1947. We left Halifax, producer Syd Kennedy, engineer Arleigh Canning, and myself, and drove to Wedgeport by way of the Annapolis Valley. It was a glorious day in early September, and to my incredulous eyes, which had never encountered more than a few baskets of apples displayed in stores, the sight of that charming valley's orchards extending for miles on either side of the road as we drove was almost too much to take in all at once — hundreds of square miles of trees looking as though they might collapse at any moment under the weight of a bumper crop of Nova Scotia's world-famous apple — the firm, tart, juicy Gravenstein.

The nearest hotel accommodation to Wedgeport was in Yarmouth, a few miles away, and after checking into the Grand Hotel around midafternoon, we spent the next few hours in the crowded lobby watching the arrival of the various team members. One of the first in was Capt. Cyril Frisby, V.C., from England, who looked more like an Alec Guinness character than the captain of the British Empire team. By the time the members of the United States team and the Argentine team drifted in, the lobby of that quiet little hotel was echoing to a melange of impeccable Oxford English, a variety of hard, flat U.S. regional dialects, and rapid-fire Spanish.

However, it was the ultimate arrival of the Cuban team which really brought the place to life. The Cubans, millionaires all, were led by a huge voluble and volatile character named Thorvald Sanchez. They had come in by private plane from Havana, not sitting three abreast and reading *Ladies Home Journal* like the poor seat-belt bourgeois of Air Canada flights. These playboys of the western world luxuriated all the way in a sumptuous airborne living room with comfortable chesterfields, divans, easy chairs, and standing lamps. Sprinkled throughout the Cuban delegation was an eye-catching admixture of curvaceous Cuban cuties who were much too attentive and solicitous to their male companions to have been mere wives. From the inviting smiles and torrid glances that flashed continuously from under dark lashes, we sized them up as competitors in their own right participating in a tournament where the catch was of far greater consequence than any tuna. They were, we concluded, fishers of men.

The next morning we rose at five o'clock to cover the first day's competition, which was taking place ten miles out on the Atlantic over a stretch of water known as Soldier's Rip. We had our own CBC boat assigned to us, an open-deck Cape Islander, and with our Acadian guide at the wheel we pushed off from the jetty at Wedgeport and chugged out through the long channel that flowed between two rocky headlands to the open sea. During the slow trip out through the channel, the three of us sat huddled on a wooden seat in the stern. I was leaning against the port gunwale clutching our precious and, even then, antiquated wire recorder. A thick, chilling fog had rolled in from the open sea so that we couldn't see either of the high, barren, and rocky cliffs that bordered the channel. But when our guide veered in too close from time to time, a cluster of ominous craggy boulders would suddenly loom up only five feet off our starboard side. On such occasions our guide would give the wheel a quick yank, and we'd head back out into the opaque curtain of fog, hoping we were somewhere in the centre of the channel and not too close to the cliff on the *other* side.

We proceeded on in this fashion for about three-quarters of an hour, during which time little was spoken. Though no one would admit it, we were all preoccupied with the disquieting thought that at any moment we could strike those invisible but ever-lurking cliffs without any forewarning. To divert my mind from such gloomy thoughts, I was mentally selecting words at random to see how many words I could make from the letters of any chosen word. I had just finished with "Titanic" and was trying to see what I could do with "iceberg" when I noticed the faint outline of our guide standing a few feet in front of us. He had turned to face us and was now

33

standing with his back to the wheel, asking us over the noise of the boat's engine, "Hey, you know why dees place ees call Sojur's Keep?" We answered "no" in a thinly disguised chorus of unison boredom. He then went on to tell us that in the area there were two rip tides constantly pulling against each other, and if one were to fall into the water the suction exerted by the two opposing tidal forces would drag the unfortunate victim straight down. To illustrate this phenomenon he had used his hands, pulling them away from one another with palms upturned and fingers slightly curled. Then he nodded in the direction of a churning patch of cold green water which had suddenly appeared through the wisps of dissipating fog and volunteered: "My brudder, ee fell in dere one day. By God, ee 'ad no chance, ee wass drown jus' like dat!"

The words were scarcely out of his mouth when we heard the shuddering crunch of our wooden keel trying to grind its way over a submerged rock. The next thing we knew, the boat was teetering on its port side, making almost a complete right angle to the water with about three inches of freeboard showing above the waterline. I found myself hanging out over the gunwale still clinging to the cumbersome old wire recorder and trying to keep it from sinking out of sight. It was already half submerged and my face was about an inch above the water. It was impossible to straighten up because the full weight of Syd Kennedy and Arleigh Canning was sprawled on top of me where they'd been flung by the impact. I couldn't believe it was still the same day when the boat finally concluded its precarious balancing act and decided to fall back the way it had come instead of completing its flip. The second it had righted itself our guide rushed to lift up the deck hatch and check for leaks. Fortunately, there were none, and we were able to push on out into the Atlantic with no further bother except the guide's entreating us over his shoulder every two minutes, "You don' say nudding 'bout dees on da radio. I lose my job and dat's for sure!"

Later that evening when we had returned to our hotel room in Yarmouth and were hard put to fill an ad-libbed half-hour report to the network on what had been a rather uneventful day of fishing, we were strongly tempted to pad with the story of our near-disaster. However, we kept Mr. Boudreau's secret locked within our breasts and, if he hasn't since hung himself up on another submerged rock, I believe the man is still serving as a guide in the present day tournaments.

The second day of the tournament was much more exciting from a fishing point of view. We hadn't been out on the Rip an hour, bobbing up and down monotonously on the swell, when we spotted one of the Cuban boats flying the white flag from its mast, the signal that a strike had been made. We gunned our engine and headed over to the scene. As we got within hailing distance, they told us that the Cuban captain, Thorvald Sanchez, had what was believed to be at least an eight hundred pounder on the line. There was old Thorvald, sure enough, his face beet-red and dripping with perspiration, reeling in his line for all he was worth, the ridiculously flimsy rod bent almost into the shape of a hairpin. Two guides were standing by the gunwale with gaffs at the ready, but at the moment we had no glimpse of the big bluefin which was fighting for his life somewhere down in the depths of the Atlantic at the end of that line. A third guide had now moved up to Thorvald's swivel chair and was mopping off the perspiration with a towel. Still no sign of that invisible phantom which was the cause of all Thorvald's grunts, groans, gasps, and rivulets of sweat.

Suddenly, about a hundred feet off the stern rail where Thorvald had braced his big Cuban boots for additional leverage, there was a momentary eddying, a lightning flash of white foam and spray, and out of the vortex, in a great spasmodic leap, came eight hundred pounds of dark blue carcass. Up and out he went over the water before arching into a powerful dive that took him out of sight again. The leviathan was trying to sound — the last magnificent and desperate gesture of scorn which a tuna often makes to avoid the humility of being relentlessly reeled in — a calculated suicidal smash into the ocean floor. On board the Cuban boat the counter strategy was to reel in furiously, to shorten the line as quickly as possible, to arrest and divert the downward momentum, veering him away from the ocean floor and into an arc-like course that would bring him still closer to the waiting gaffs.

It was all over in another ten minutes, and half a dozen gaffs reached over the gunwale as he came alongside, hooked him, and inched him up and over with a great sodden thump onto the deck. With the wire recorder going, I was giving a running commentary as I threw a leg over our boat and into the Cuban boat. I started along the deck of the Cuban boat to where the monster, looking twice as large lying there in his incongruous new environment, was stretched out motionless. My sympathies were with the loser, and I remember babbling into the recorder about "that huge baleful eye staring up accusingly at all of us". The personification was rudely interrupted by the sudden sweep of an Acadian guide's arm, which pushed me back away from the tuna, and a shouted warning that one convulsive whip of that tuna's tail could send me and my CBC recorder flying out over the rail of the boat. I then gave the tuna a wide margin and made my way down the deck to where Thorvald was slumped in his chair like a limp rag doll. The interview consisted of three succinct words, offered up in a hoarse gasp, which we later sent out to the network that evening," I ... am ... pooped."

By midafternoon of that second day, white flags seemed to be flying from masts all over that area of the Atlantic, as boat after boat began to get strikes. In our CBC boat we'd scurry from one proud competitor to another, recording pretty much the same "It was a tough fight but I'm glad I won" sort of comment. However, when I scrambled into the boat where Captain Cyril Frisby, V.C., sat calmly surveying the monster he'd just landed as if it were a lake trout, I got quite a different response. My initial question concerning the estimated weight of his tuna triggered off a half-hour lecture on the correct pronunciation of the word "tuna".

"You North Americans insist on pronouncing it 'tyoo-na' but at home, of course, it's always 'tunny' and I think we're a jolly sight more correct." Then, as we sat slowly bobbing up and down on the swell ten miles out in the Atlantic, he went on to remind me, "When you recall that in the original Latin

root, *tunnis,* the penultimate vowel precedes a double consonant, you must admit that the short vowel sound is called for
rather than the long." When I was eventually dismissed, I
backed up over the side and rejoined my crass fellow coloni-
als in the CBC boat feeling as flat and deflated as Jack Dempsey when he was knocked out by Gene Tuna.

The Acadian fishermen who lived around Wedgeport and
who were hired as guides for the tournament each year did
very well for themselves during the few days that the competition lasted. In addition to the hundred dollars a day they
were paid for their services, they were also allowed to keep
all the tuna that were caught. But to these men who fished
commercially, the whole idea of men sitting for hours, killing
themselves trying to boat a giant bluefin for sport with rod
and line, was a topic of great amusement. I asked our guide,
Mr. Boudreau, how they caught their tuna. "We get a big hoil
drum," he explained, "den we tie six, seven line to dat drum
wit hooks. Den we bait da hooks wit 'erreen and trow da
drum over da side. Pretty soon da drum she stop moveen.
We know den dat big feesh can't pull no more, got no more
fight. We go pull him in da boat."

On the last day of the tournament as we cruised around
Soldier's Rip looking for action, we got word that one of the
Cuban team members was about a mile away, fighting to boat
a monstrous tuna which all the seasoned guides were esti-
mating to be well over one thousand pounds. He was the local
Moby Dick, who had been sighted from time to time in the
area but who had managed, so far, to evade capture. When we
arrived alongside the Cuban boat we could see Julio Sanchez,
Thorvald's nephew, slowly and with great physical strain
reeling in a few feet of line at a time and pausing between
efforts to have the perspiration wiped out of his eyes. It took
him an hour or more to inch the big fish to within gaffing distance of the boat, where according to tournament regulations
he could at last relax and turn the tuna over to the guides for
the actual landing. We watched three or four gaffs bite into
the massive dark blue back that was now breaking the surface
like the hull of a U-boat. Julio, confident that his prize was

37

secure and his ordeal over, was sprawled in his swivel chair, chest heaving and arms hanging limply at his sides.

Suddenly, two of the gaffs cracked in two under the strain of hoisting such a dead weight, and the formerly passive leviathan made the most of his reprieve. With a whoosh he took off like a bullet, and by the time the startled Julio had lunged for his rod on the decking, the tuna had pulled off at least a mile of loose line. The job had to begin again from scratch. Two hours later Julio, with glazed eyes and ashen face, was still straining to regain a few feet of line at a time. We had to turn our CBC boat around and head for our hotel room in Yarmouth because of two broadcasts we had to do early that evening, and so reluctantly we left poor old Julio to battle on without knowing what the outcome would be.

At six o'clock that evening, back in our hotel room, Syd Kennedy finished his broadcast report on the day's events to the Trans Canada Network. Half an hour later I went on the air for a fifteen-minute report to the Caribbean through the CBC's international short-wave facilities. Syd sat about two feet away from me as I ad-libbed my way through the broadcast. With about two minutes left to go, I launched into an account of the titanic struggle going on at that very moment out on Soldier's Rip between Julio Sanchez and what was believed to be the largest tuna ever sighted in Maritime waters. The ad-lib report was rolling out very nicely, but in the back of my mind I was mentally searching for just the right kind of clincher sentence to round out my report. Without thinking I said, "I don't know if Julio is going to land that giant tuna but I can tell you one thing, if Julio doesn't get that fish, well, he just won't come back."

I then delivered the CBC cue and, feeling rather proud of myself, glanced over at Syd just in time to see his mouth drop open and emit a long, anguished groan. He then clasped one hand to his forehead in a gesture of desperation and slid slowly off his chair onto the hotel-room floor. "Jeez, what a helluva line to send down to the Caribbean. If Julio doesn't get that fish he just won't come back. I'll bet his poor family down in Havana are going up the wall just about now." Syd then went on to predict that the Sanchez family would be lighting candles in cathedrals all over Havana for Julio's safety, "all on account of you and that goddam line."

It wasn't until half-past ten that same evening when the prizes were being awarded at the closing banquet that Julio was dragged through the hotel dining room on his way to his room by two guides in oilskins who had him under each armpit. His head lolled over drunkenly onto one shoulder and his feet, with the toes turned in, dragged limply along the floor behind him. But he was home, albeit without the tuna, and Kennedy began talking to me again.

One of the first program duties I can recall performing after my arrival at CBC Halifax was inserting the all important surf and seagull cries into the body of the Sunday morning program, *Harmony Harbour*. While the organist, Marjorie Payne, the Acadian Male Quartet, and the narrator, Syd Kennedy, all gave of their best in the ballroom of the Nova Scotian Hotel, I sat a couple of miles away in the main CBC studios on Sackville Street with a sound-effects record of surf and gulls poised on the turntable beside me. With a copy of the script in front of me I was able to follow the narration and also listen to it by means of earphones. Whenever I came across the bracketed cue, SURF AND GULLS, my job was to let the record go and regulate the volume so that the surf and gull sounds would enhance the narrator's prose without being intrusive.

It was pointed out to me by the other announcers at the very outset that the monotony of this task could be relieved by making a little game of it. The object of the game was to see how thoroughly each time one could drown out the narrator's voice with the surf and gulls. The narrator was Syd Kennedy. He'd been the voice of this popular Sunday morning network program for years, and even though he was at that time manager of the Halifax station, he jealously guarded this prestige assignment from the regular announcers and made sure that each Sunday his was the Lorelei voice which tugged at the hearts of exiled Maritimers all across Canada with that familiar opening siren call:

And inland, where the dark hills rise
Between you and the salt-thick foam
You hear the surf — the seagulls' cries
And Eastward, turn your hearts toward home.

It would have been difficult, of course, for a narrator to have missed with the magnificent and moving prose which Frank W. Doyle, a Halifax newspaper editor, wrote for those *Harmony Harbour* broadcasts. It had the Joseph Conrad touch and read like a musical score. The subject material, drawn from the Maritimes' historical past, did, however, have a slightly lugubrious quality. It dealt mostly with the shipwrecks and the incursions made against early Maritimes settlements by marauding Indians, French, and New England privateers. It seemed that almost every anecdote ended with such lines as, "... and with a mournful shudder the *Brenda Marie* went to the bottom, taking with her 108 souls who were never to see their home port again," or,

"... putting the entire village to the torch, slaughtering 112 of its inhabitants, and then making off overland with 140 wretched survivors who were never again to see their native land." This proclivity of *Harmony Harbour* for disaster prompted one unfeeling Toronto radio critic to write in his column, "Having listened to *Harmony Harbour* since it began, I've now been able to compute that an average of 420 poor souls have been either drowned, massacred, or carried off every Sunday morning for the past fifteen years. How in hell can there be anyone left down there?"

For a period of nearly a month, Syd Kennedy almost succeeded in undermining our little diversion of drowning out his voice with surf and gulls every Sunday morning. As he read his script to the network from the CBC's Nova Scotian Hotel studios, he hit upon the counterstrategy of anticipating our inserted sound effects from the main studios a mile away. Consequently, whenever he approached to within a sentence or two of the underlined cue, SURF AND GULLS, he would start "building" — increasing his voice in volume and intensity

40

— so that try as we would, with our surf and gull effects going at full blast over his voice, there was always a tiny but audible vestige of a thin, shrieking human voice cutting through.

His triumph was short-lived. Some unsung Leonardo of the Halifax announce staff whose name I've forgotten suggested that on such occasions when Kennedy anticipated, we would refrain completely from putting in any surf and gulls whatever. The resulting effect was most rewarding — ten times more hilarious than our former attempts to drown him out. I'm quite sure that thousands of unwitting listeners, in the privacy of their living rooms across Canada, must have been stunned by that screaming Hitler-like voice shouting its message of doom and disaster and must have felt that Kennedy was holding them all personally responsible for those poor devils who were in the process of being "carried off, never to see their native land again". I can still see the Grand Old Man of Radio, as we used to call him, bursting into Studio B every Sunday morning about four minutes after Harmony Harbour had gone off the air. This was the approximate time it took him to race from the ballroom of the Nova Scotian Hotel, leap into the CBC staff car, and come screaming up to our main Sackville Street studios to confront me with a wild outburst of profanity just as I was sheepishly putting away my surf and gulls record for another week.

It's a dubious honour, I realize, but in all my years to date I've heard no one who could handle profanity as effectively or imaginatively as the Grand Old Man of Radio. I'm told that some Australians, given a basic four-letter Anglo-Saxon word, can use it in the same sentence as verb, subject, object, and adverb. Kennedy had no such limitations. Given any profane root, Kennedy, when pushed, could not only use it as the basic main parts of speech but, through a nimble interplay of prefixes and suffixes, could ad lib a five-minute tirade of shockingly exotic gerunds, gerundives, expletives, and participles — everything, in fact, except prepositions. There wasn't much that even Syd could do with "by, in, at, to," and they always seemed to stand out as sore thumbs in an otherwise flawless performance. Today, S.R. Kennedy is the cue's Regional Director for the Maritimes and as far as I'm concerned has only one other talent — that of being the most knowledgeable, efficient, and popular senior executive in the entire corporation.

III

IT WAS SOMEWHERE in the dying weeks of December, 1946, that Old Rawhide was born and rose, more like a Quasimodo than a Phoenix, from the ashes of the old year. As the newest addition to the announce staff of CBC Halifax, I took my turn at all the various assignments in the normal program day — newscaster, host of record shows, farm broadcast announcer, wet nurse to women commentators and, of course, surf and gull man on Harmony Harbour. At the end of my second week, I reported for duty on a Saturday morning, checked my schedule of duties and found to my horror that they included a half hour of cowboy records called *After Breakfast Breakdown*. With the exception of a very few legitimate songs which were actually sung by cowboys and have come down to us from the old frontier days of the American west, I loathe the entire field of Tin Pan Alley hokum loosely termed "cowboy music". Moreover, at twenty-one I was a good bit more impressionable than I am now and being a fully fledged CBC announcer was to me, at least in those days, only a rank or two below beatification. I had already blabbed all over Halifax to any who would listen the long list of vital and indispensable duties with which I had been entrusted by the CBC. What on earth would these people think now if they should hear me feigning an enthusiastic introduction to some guitar-twanging drugstore cowboy singing, "I Rapped On the Hearse Window, Granny, But You Did Not Look Out", or something of similar inspiration.

With a desperation born of despair and with just twenty seconds to air time, I hit on the idea of disguising my voice by dropping the register, thrusting out my jaw, and clamping my back teeth together. As I pushed down the microphone switch, out came the words, "Howdy! Welcome to *After Breakfast Breakdown,*" in a low, aged, hard, flat, sloppily sibilant voice that surprised even myself. "This is your old pal Rawhide," I continued, pulling the name out of the air on the spur of the moment, although I'd heard it used once or twice in my life to denote a type of tough, untanned leather. I then proceeded for the next half hour to introduce each cowboy record in the most insulting fashion I could devise, popping in at the close of each song to thank the artist and bid him farewell as he "mosied off down the canyon, headin' tall in the saddle into the flaming sunset, whose glare would no doubt prevent him from seeing in time that 400-foot sheer drop into the chasm below waiting to claim him for that great Studio in the Sky ... and not a moment too soon."

The names of the various cowboy singers were all strange to my ears (as were the voices) and so, when I cued up the second last record that morning and noticed that the performer was billed as the Yodelling Ranger, I didn't think it would be too indiscreet to good-naturedly change this in my introduction to the Yodelling Idiot. The record finished, and I thanked him, sending him on his way to the Great Studio in the Sky via the 400-foot chasm I'd so felicitously invented. Suddenly the studio door opened slightly, and there was Syd Kennedy's panic-stricken face mouthing some message which, though I couldn't decipher it, nevertheless seemed quite urgent. The thought crossed my mind as I was trying to lip-read Syd and at the same time verbally despatch the Yodelling Idiot that perhaps the studios were on fire. I quickly sent the Yodelling Idiot over the cliff, released the last record of the program without any introduction, and cut my microphone.

At last I was able to ask Syd what the problem was. He took two full minutes to babble out his message, but when I'd mentally pruned all the extraneous and profane prefixes and suffixes it was reduced to a rather concise skeletal form — "The Yodelling Ranger is not only a local Halifax boy but also the most popular idol in the Maritimes." Syd further advised that, to avoid being lynched the moment I stepped out onto Sackville Street, I should hastily make the most abject apology I could think of. There wasn't much program time left, so I faded down the record that was playing, opened my microphone, and said, still in the Rawhide voice, "I just made a very unfortunate mistake in calling that previous singer the Yodelling Idiot. I certainly didn't mean to be disparaging and was obviously confusing him with *another* Yodelling Idiot I once knew in Upper Canada. This is the Canadian Broadcasting Corporation."

Kennedy showed great restraint, waiting till the very last word of the corporation cue was finished and the microphone cut before he clasped both hands to his head, emitted an anguished groan, and vanished from the studio. His fears were quite unfounded. It must have been my juxtaposition of the words "idiot" and "Upper Canada" which appeased the aficionados of the cowboy idiom in Halifax. At any rate the apology was accepted as a complete and penitent catharsis, and I was to reach my little rented room that day without being set upon by an unruly mob.

The chief danger to my well-being was to come a few days later from a different and totally unexpected source, S.R. Kennedy. I was called into his office at the beginning of the following week to face what I presumed would be nothing more than a mild lecture on the importance of being kind to local cowboy singers. However, it turned out that Syd had completely forgotten my faux pas in the excitement of a brilliant idea he'd conceived over the weekend and which was now beginning to spring fully formed, *mirabile dictu*, from his mouth. "I like the idea of using that old guy's voice. Starting next Monday, we're scheduling a half hour of cowboy music, six mornings a week, to the Maritime network with you as host doing the old guy's voice!"

I can remember, once my speech returned, trying to reason with Syd. I was being quite serious when I offered to do extra announce shifts and even give the CBC one night a week janitorial service if he'd only abandon this insane idea. But it was like asking a mother to abandon her firstborn, and though I continued to plead and protest, Syd merely sat, smiling smugly like a balding Mona Lisa, gazing out through his office window at his favourite landmark, the red funnels of the old *Aquitania* thrusting up from the harbour. The following Monday I reluctantly launched the first program in a series that was to run for seventeen consecutive years.

Whereas most broadcasters strive either to entertain or inform, my motivation during those early weeks of incarceration on the Devil's Island to which Kennedy had sent me was considerably more selfish. It was simply to make that half hour of cowboy music each morning pass as quickly and painlessly as possible. Not knowing or caring who might be listening and strictly for my own amusement, I brought into the studio with me each morning a little sound-effects door. Between cowboy records I would open and close this door to signal the arrival of mythical characters and, one by one, I would people my little cell with quite an assortment of warped figments of my imagination to keep me company.

There was Granny, her sweet little eggshell voice giving no indication of the thoroughly rotten, corrupt, and malicious personality which lurked behind it. There was Marvin Mellobell, a sickeningly irritating embodiment of all the adenoids, pomposity, and self-adulation that the world of show-biz had to offer. Then there was my favourite, the unnamed pest and constant thorn in Marvin Mellobell's flesh, whose wild, semi-literate speech poured out in the raucous voice of Doug Trowell's old Scott C. Mulsion. He was a sort of Rousseau's natural man carried to the extreme, unfettered by even the thinnest veneer of social decorum. What he lacked in polish and mentality he made up for in enthusiasm and in his time played all the major roles in the Rawhide Little Theatre Company. From Tarzan of the Apes to the brooding Prince of Denmark, they all rolled out with the same raw gusto and paucity of dramatic insight.

There were also the Goomer Brothers, rural entrepreneurs who operated an illicit hard-cider operation in the Gaspereau district of Nova Scotia's lovely Annapolis Valley. They hated the RCMP and were constantly and angrily campaigning on the program to get the CBC to include, along with road and weather reports, Mountie Reports designed to keep the little man in their particular field posted on the latest whereabouts of the federal law. They also purveyed as a sideline 155 over-proof eggs derived from a flock of semi-stoned White Leghorns which they fed on fermenting apple mash. Their steady customers included world-famous personalities who unwittingly bit into the free trial samples which the Goomer Brothers mailed out all over the world and became hopelessly hooked. The only sample egg ever to be returned unopened was the one they sent Princess Margaret Rose, and she was immediately lumped in with the RCMP as their favourite objects of scorn and dislike.

Rawhide often feigned horror at some of the things all these characters came out with, but secretly he, and certainly his creator, welcomed these morning visits and prolonged them, knowing full well they were eating up valuable time which otherwise would have to be devoted to the cowboy records. Although these little interludes with character voices served as welcome and selfishly devised breaks in the monotony, I never for a moment lost sight of my main objective in those early weeks. I continued to wait patiently for the opportunity to get myself taken off the air.

It was a good six weeks before the golden moment arrived in the form of a nasty letter from some lady in New Brunswick who was taking violent umbrage at what she alleged was my blatant partiality toward Wilf Carter and the shameful neglect of Hank Snow. These men were the two top favourites in the Maritimes in the field of cowboy music. Like a mother striving to avoid sibling rivalry, I meticulously played one record of each singer every single morning, except on one occasion while possibly wool-gathering, when I allowed a second Wilf Carter aria to slip in at the expense of Hank Snow. It was this occasion to which she was referring in her letter. I read the letter through to myself twice, scarcely able to believe, from the strength of the language, that it had been penned by one of the weaker sex. However, for what I had in mind she'd do nicely. Dreyfus had found his Zola.

The very next morning, instead of opening with the usual camaraderie, I asked the operator in the control room to play a particularly heartrending version of *Hearts and Flowers.* Then

I came in over this as Rawhide, with much sniffling and nose-blowing, to say in a shaken voice, "In the short time I've been living in these parts, I've come to look upon Marimtiders as a friendly, warm-hearted bunch, and it saddens my old heart this morning to realize there's one among you who is trying to cut my throat behind my back." I then read the letter verbatim (omitting only the pungent parts) and ended with the writer's name, street address, and home town. Then I went on, "You realize, of course, Mrs. — of — Street in —, New Brunswick, that I would be quite within my rights to say something nasty to you in return. But somehow, deep down inside, I'm ... well ... I'm just not built that way. Instead, I'm merely going to turn the other cheek and ask you, in the spirit of true Christian friendship to (here I paused for dramatic effect) ... *drop dead!*"

The expression in those days was just coming into vogue and had not yet lost its freshness and shock value through later overuse. It must have sounded particularly fresh when boomed over a 50,000-watt transmitter to a CBC customer who at the time was no doubt paying her $2.50 licence fee to help keep the likes of me on the air. There was no doubt in my mind that she would be justifiably outraged and would contact her local MP in Ottawa who, in turn, would contact the Minister of Transport. Next in the chain of command would be A. Davidson Dunton, then chairman of the CBC Board of Governors, who would call W.E.S. Briggs, who would take me off the program. Like the old lady's cow, I'd be over the stile and home free. Two days later my house of cards collapsed when the woman wrote me again to say, "Well, Rawhide, old pal you sure gave it to me over the air the other day and by golly I asked for it. No hard feelings."

Along about this time the Rawhide program had begun to bring in a rather steady flow of mail from all over the Atlantic provinces. From these letters I began to realize that there was an encouraging percentage of the audience who were listening for the skits I was doing and not the cowboy records. My morale picked up. Earlier, the mail had consisted almost entirely of requests for cowboy songs, usually of the more

morbid variety. One lady, writing with soft pencil in a most la-
borious and semi-legible hand had requested *We Shall Gather
By the River* sung by the Carter Family, "in memory of my
daughter that was drowned there six years ago."

The mail each day would invariably bring several parcels,
sometimes chocolates or home-made cookies, but most often
sturdy knitted mittens or toques from Newfoundland. Among
the many pairs of heavy-duty white wool socks that were
knitted and sent in by ladies in Newfoundland was one pair
which came in with the instruction, "Wear these over your
shoes to save the leather." On my CBC salary of nineteen
hundred dollars a year I can assure you that none of these
gifts was sneezed at.

For well over a year, few listeners in the Maritimes had any
idea who this old codger, Rawhide, really was or where he came
from. Most were convinced he really was an old man. Even as
late as 1952, when I'd been doing the program out of Toronto
for three years, the CBC program people received a letter from
an elderly people's club in Toronto saying that, although they
appreciated what the CBC was trying to do for old folks in
keeping Rawhide working, really he'd been on for more than
his share, and there were a couple of octogenarian piano players who would like to take over his program spot. One letter
I'll always remember from those early Maritime days was the
one sent in by a dear old soul living in one of the outports of
Newfoundland. She enclosed with the letter a snap of herself
sitting with her arm around a sheep with an out-house in the
background, and from this I judged her to be certainly in her
late seventies. She confessed that there was a kindly quality in
old Rawhide's voice, and she felt that she would like to share
her twilight years with him. In all the seventeen years I
was to carry on the imposture, this was the only incident that
made me feel a twinge of guilt, and I found it very difficult,
in my reply to her, to have to shatter love's old dream with the
disclosure that old Rawhide was twenty-two.

No performer could have wished for a more good-na-
tured or responsive audience than those Maritime listeners
of some twenty years ago who had the "growing pains" of

the Rawhide show to contend with. They reacted with more enthusiasm than I deserved to those early and rather crudely conceived skits which I served them up each morning. The extent to which they went along with the nonsense sometimes amazed me. An example of this listener participation would be the week "little Harold" was carted off to hospital. "Little Harold" was an imaginary Black Widow spider who used to be brought in occasionally to visit Rawhide by his imaginary owner — an ominously gentle character cast in the vocal mould of the late Peter Lorre. Harold, his beloved pet, was a sullen, bad-tempered, vicious brute who, like an entomological Heathcliff, would repay any word of kindness addressed to him by sinking his venomous little fangs into the offender. One morning he made the mistake of going for Granny, who promptly felled him with one vicious blow of her rolled-up brolly and then proceeded to jump up and down on him with old-fashioned high-button boots. It was a busy moment for me. As Granny, I had to emit angry little phrases such as, "Take that you cheeky little monkey!" As Harold's owner I had to plead with Granny to stop pulverizing Harold, and as Rawhide I had to try to separate and placate all three protagonists. All the while, I attempted to suggest Harold's painful predicament by slowly crushing a quart berry box with my hands. Harold's tiny cries of pain were produced by pursing my lips together tightly and forcing air through, which resulted in a series of minute, semi-audible squeaks. Fortunately, for the sound of an ambulance arriving, I was able to rely on a sound-effect record played from the control room by my operator. The episode ended with two orderlies from the Victoria General Hospital in Halifax carrying off the mangled body of little Harold on a stretcher.

For the next few days Rawhide would read out progress bulletins on the state of Harold's condition as he lay on his little bed of pain at the VG. An imaginary doctor popped in to the studio one day, having left Harold unattended just long enough to be interviewed by Rawhide and speak with glowing admiration of this "plucky little patient who had bravely ignored his multiple fracture and spun his own oxygen tent."

I couldn't believe my eyes when dozens of get-well cards began coming in for this nonexistent spider. Even more incredible were the several miniature suits which came in for Harold, intricately and painstakingly knitted. Among the food parcels which came in, there arrived one morning a small cardboard box with ominous-looking air holes punched in the top. Inside was a live praying mantis and the message, "Just in case Harold gets tired of the hospital food."

How different was to be the peevish, ill-humoured reaction I was to get several years later when I involved the Toronto General Hospital in a skit of similar vein. On this occasion, my skit was promoted by the newspaper item that Russian doctors had successfully transplanted one dog's head onto the body of another, and that the world's first manmade,

Max, performing Harold the Spider.

two-headed dog was doing nicely. Granny and the raucous-voiced character immediately saw in this a wonderful way to save the CBC money. "Why couldn't several performers' heads," they asked with their customary astuteness, "be grafted onto a single body, thereby necessitating only one performing fee and reducing the drain on the CBC's program budget?" Their compelling argument was that the saving involved would bring coloured TV that much closer.

Mindful of the need to walk before they ran, they began by modestly attempting to graft James Bannerman's head onto Ma Perkins' body. Ma, I need hardly explain, was the currently reigning diva of the afternoon soap serials — a rather loathsome old goody two-shoes who was hell bent on bringing sunshine into the lives of everyone she met, whether they wanted it or not. As the locale for this particular skit, I unwittingly chose an operating room in the Toronto General. Against a background noise of sawing and sewing machines, a horrified Marvin Mellobell attempted to conduct a proper CBC interview with the pair. As they sewed and sawed, with Granny whimsically humming away to herself, the raucous-voiced one explained in gory detail some of the difficulties they had encountered. The chief difficulty turned out to be that James Bannerman's neck arteries were 60 gauge, 15 denier, whereas old Ma's were only 50 gauge, 10 denier. The dramatic highlight of the broadcast was to be the actual voices of the two human guinea pigs being questioned by Marvin after they came out of the anaesthetic. There was gripping tension in Marvin's voice as he leaned over the two-headed form on the operating table. With slow, deliberate enunciation he asked, "How ... do ... you ... feel?"

James Bannerman's voice was the first to reply, "Land o'Goshen, child, just wonderful!"

This was followed immediately by the whining voice of Ma Perkins saying, "Good evening and welcome to CBC Wednesday Night."

The skit ended with Marvin fighting back nausea while the raucous-voiced character seized the two recuperative heads by the throat, shook them violently, and screamed at them hysterically, "Speak proper, youse rotten ingrates! Don't youse play smart alec with me! Speak, I say Speak!" This sketch resulted in my being summoned three days later to the office of Captain Briggs — CBC Maritime Regional Director. "Did you recently involve Toronto General Hospital in one of your skits?" I admitted I had. "In what connection?" he pursued. I then explained that I had needed a well-equipped and reputable operating room in which some of my characters could graft James Bannerman's head onto Ma Perkins body. Briggs winced. "I've just had Davidson Dunton on the phone from Ottawa," he said. "Apparently some of the members of the hospital board are giving Dunton a hard time. They want a public apology from you."

This was to be the one and only occasion in Rawhide's seventeen years on the air when he had to eat crow. It turned out, however, to be quite a palatable meal. The very next morning Rawhide explained to the audience what had happened and took full responsibility for any embarrassment occasioned the Toronto General Hospital. "We had originally intended to do the operation a little farther down University Avenue at Quong Lee's Hand Laundry, but, due to an unfortunate mistake in address, ended up at the Toronto General. It's a fine hospital, and if I'm ever pregnant again, I certainly won't hesitate to have my baby there."

Briggs came up to me in the studio corridor later that day. "I didn't catch the show this morning, but I assume you made the apology?"

"Abjectly," I assured him.

"Good show," he replied and contentedly lumbered off. I often wonder how much CBC official censure or even divine wrath I might have brought down around my ears in those Halifax days had my long-cherished dream ever materialized. Quite early in my Rawhide career I conceived what I thought was a wonderful line to put into Rawhide's mouth some morning at the opening of the Rawhide program. I carried it in the back of my mind for over three years, hoping for the auspicious morning when all the circumstances necessary for the effective delivery of the line would be present at the same moment.

I got the idea for this memorable line one morning when I was assigned to the devotional program which immediately preceded the Rawhide show. The guest minister on that particular morning was a gentleman by the name of Reverend Pentz. He was a local Halifax minister who, along other guest ministers, would turn up from time to time on *Morning Devotions* to deliver a brief sermon or read from the Bible. As the minutes ticked by and Reverend Pentz showed no signs of winding up his sermon, I began to fidget and wonder would there be time for me to sign him off, deliver the CBC cue, and get down the hall to Studio C in time to start my Rawhide program.

It was then that I suddenly thought of that golden moment for which I patiently waited three years and which never did arrive; a morning when Reverend Pentz would be the guest minister on *Morning Devotions,* when he would choose to round off the program with the reading of the Twenty-third Psalm, when through an oversight on his part, he would go beyond the allotted time and spill over into the Rawhide show, forcing Rawhide to start late. *Then* old Rawhide would be able to come in with the opening line, "Pentz, you made the psalm too long." However, it never came about, and perhaps it is just as well.

One day late in 1948, after two full years had passed without Maritime listeners gaining any inkling as to Rawhide's identity or background, the cat was let out of the bag in one fell swoop. On the morning in question the CBC Regional Engineer for the Maritimes, H.M. Smith, was paying one of his periodic visits to the Halifax studios from his base in Sackville, New Brunswick, where he kept a competent eye on our 50,000-watt domestic transmitter. He was also in charge of the sprawling network of antennas which beamed the Voice of Canada to all parts of the world. I used to tease him fairly regularly on the Rawhide program. Rawhide always referred to him as Marconi Moe and made disparaging remarks about the "few hundred yards of waxed string and honey pails which he fobbed off on everyone as the CBC's short-wave operation".

Knowing "Moe" was somewhere around the studios that morning, Rawhide was busily engaged in explaining to the listeners that what Marconi Moe really did to get Canadian programs to the world was to roll up the scripts, put them in bottles, and toss them into the Gulf Stream.

Suddenly in the middle of all this teasing, there was a bright flash of light through the control room glass. Moe Smith had slipped into the control room and snapped my picture. I don't know why it bothered me (especially after the Doug Trowell days), but I was genuinely startled and flustered. I jumped up, pushing my chair back noisily, and still managing to hold onto the Rawhide voice I shouted, "Somebody stop Marconi Moe! Don't let him out of the building! He's just taken my picture!"

In the mail later that week there were quite a few requests for copies of that photograph that Smith had taken of old Rawhide. I answered them all evasively, but the requests began to increase in number. I then tried mentioning on the air that Rawhide shared a strange characteristic with vampires — he cast no reflection in mirrors and made no impression on negatives. This piece of evasive levity, however, had no effect on the steadily building flow of requests.

As Rawhide I'd always treasured my anonymity and felt it quite essential to the continuance of his uninhibited character. On a previous occasion I had strongly objected to a short-lived official memo which directed Halifax announcers to identify Rawhide as CBC announcer, Max Ferguson, at the close of each Rawhide program. Now, though, this new threat to the old codger's anonymity coming from the listeners themselves posed a real dilemma which I viewed with alarm.

Syd Kennedy preferred to view the situation as one of those tides in the affairs of the CBC which should be taken at the flood. He decided to bring in a local photographer to take my picture and have three thousand copies printed to be made available to listeners on request. "Probably do a composite job," he shouted over my protests, "with you, as yourself, surrounded by about four of your characters." Within three weeks the CBC in Halifax had mailed out just under 9,000 of these composite photographs.

During the three weeks, with the office boy bringing in a couple of bulging sacks of letters each morning, the entire office staff was commandeered to handle the requests. I used to take my turn at the task every morning, opening letters and filling the requests. I can remember my hysterical delight at making the discovery that just about every third letter contained a dime to handle return postage, even though the on-air announcements of the offer had made it quite clear that such a thing wasn't necessary. What wild sugar plums danced about in my greedy little head at the realization that I might well become the Elwood Glover of CBC Halifax thanks to these little love offerings. I was soon to learn, however, that I'd have to continue to make do with my salary of $1,900 per annum when the official hand of the CBC collected all those dimes and tucked them safely away in the big Corporate stock. After all the photographs had been mailed out (I looked no more than about fifteen years old in them) I realized that now at least 9,000 Maritime families knew Rawhide's well-kept secret. It may have been only my imagination, but to my ears the old boy was never to sound quite the same again. He certainly never received another marriage proposal.

Hard on the heels of this exposure came the first magazine article on the Rawhide program, written by the Maritime reporter for the *Montreal Standard,* Swifty Robinson, who described Rawhide's creator (as all ensuing articles were later to do) as "mild-mannered, unassuming CBC staff announcer, Max Ferguson". The cat was now well out of the bag.

As a Christmas present that year, 1948, the CBC offered me the chance to come to Toronto as a staff announcer and rub shoulders with such awesome names as Byng Whitteker, Elwood Glover, and Joel Aldred. The big fat goose that Scrooge lugged up the street to Tiny Tim couldn't have been more welcome. Here at last, burning before my very eyes, was the bright flame into which all CBC regional announcers dreamed one day of fluttering. In the middle of January, 1949, I arrived at the CBC Toronto studios and lasted until June, 1954 — just long enough to burn my wings to a crisp.

Mindful of how slowly the winters seem to crawl by these days before summer rolls round and I can dash from Toronto to my therapeutic haven on the rugged northern tip of Cape Breton, it seems difficult to understand the great elation I felt back in 1949 at the thought of being transferred to Toronto. However, it was early in my career and, like most young announcers starting out in the CBC regions, I regarded Toronto as the Valhalla of radio where all the great gods of the broadcasting world reposed, the envied Round Table from which broadcasters errant went forth to cover themselves in glory through the performance of noble and worthwhile feats. Legends of great moments in broadcasting had already drifted down from Toronto to Halifax to fire my imagination and ambition, like the ancient tales of mariners that lured young boys to sea, and I longed to be part of them.

For example, I could see in my mind's eye that intrepid team of professionals who set out from CBC Toronto in the late thirties to bring to a breathlessly awaiting nation the historic and horrendous crash of the old Honeymoon Bridge, which used to stand on the site of the present day Rainbow Bridge. Throughout early spring huge cakes of ice had been building up in the Niagara River, and the tremendous and inexorable pressure created by this ice mass against the foundation of the bridge meant that the end was near at hand. Fond memories of this romantic old landmark were treasured in the hearts of so many thousands of Canadians that the Canadian Broadcasting Corporation wanted to make sure that the tragic sound of its final agonies was brought to Canadians across the land. A producer, a couple of engineers, suitable recording equipment, and an announcer were sent forth to the scene. They established a base camp right beside the bridge and they waited. The minutes became hours, the hours became days, but in view of the important responsibility with which they were charged all thoughts of personal comfort were forgotten. They ate and slept on the job with their recording equipment at the ready.

Finally, on either the third or fourth day, the tantalizing

At CBC Headquarters, 354 Jarvis Street, Toronto

silhouette of the General Brock Hotel, looming up in the distance like a mocking symbol of all the warmth and comfort they'd been denied, proved too seductive a siren call for even these stalwarts to deny. There hadn't been a whimper from the bridge and it looked as solid as ever. Surely, they reasoned, a quick nip over to the Brock for a hastily gulped cup of warm coffee couldn't possibly be misconstrued as a dereliction of duty. Minutes later, in the warm and cosy atmosphere of the General Brock, cups of steaming coffee were rising to meet eager lips. And then it happened. Somewhere halfway between saucer and mouth the cups and the hands which held them were frozen into immobility by a brain-numbing, ear-splitting roar from the direction of the river below. The Honeymoon Bridge had decided not to wait for the CBC.

Nurtured on legends such as this, it was small wonder back in 1949 that I felt such an irresistible compulsion to become part of this worthwhile and meaningful CBC Toronto adventure.

IV

IN PREPARATION FOR my sojourn in this new, urbane, and polished land of gracious living that was CBC Toronto, I was careful to discard such bucolic accoutrements of my East Coast days as my cigarette roller that rolled five at once. The first person around the studios to whom I offered my new status symbol, a slickly packaged deck of ready-mades, was an executive of the Trans Canada Network. He declined with thanks, confiding that he really preferred the ones he turned out himself on a wonderful new machine he'd just discovered that could roll five at one time. The second person to whom I offered my ready-mades, with all the pride of E.P. Taylor opening his front door to guests, was Earl Cameron, voice of the CBC National News. It turned out that Earl not only disdained all ready-made cigarettes, but even scorned the effete practise of rolling cigarettes with the aid of mechanical devices. Earl rolled by hand. That first glimpse of him sitting in a little news studio wearing old denims held up by firemen's braces and spilling dry makings down the front of his rumpled woollen shirt came as a bit of a shock. For years, in my mind's eye, I had somehow pictured Earl in a long, flowing biblical robe reading the National News from a still-smouldering stone tablet. Nowadays, of course, when I watch young people sitting at Earl's feet and confessing their psychotic compulsion to divide into two groups before brushing their teeth, he seems to have approached, sartorially at least, much closer to that original father image I had of him.

An even greater disillusion than Earl Cameron's informal radio attire was waiting for me at the end of my second week round the CBC Toronto studios. After being summoned to the office of the head of the Trans Canada Network, I learned that they had brought me to Toronto not so much as a successor to Lorne Greene, but as Rawhide. The decision-makers had just finished reading all about the old fellow in the write-up that had just come out in the *Montreal Standard* and had decided to originate the Rawhide program from Toronto to the Eastern Network (Ontario and Quebec) as well as to the Maritime Network. They searched through the complicated network schedule to try to find a half-hour spot for the Rawhide program in the mornings and finally decided to remove a program called *Musical March Past* and insert Rawhide in its place. At the time it was an easy mistake to make and no one could have really foreseen the hornets' nest of protest that such a decision was soon to stir up.

Musical March Past had been on the air since the day the last little Havergal girl had scampered out of 354 Jarvis Street in her blue gym bloomers and the CBC, with its customary predilection for musty old buildings, had moved in. It was a half hour of martial music, interspersed with the voice of Peter Dawson singing either *In a Monastery Garden* or *They're Changing Guard At Buckingham Palace.* At the decision of the CBC, its millennium ended abruptly one Friday morning, and on the following Monday morning, February 14, the gravel voice of old Rawhide and those of all his demented cronies was sent out, like a grotesque CBC valentine, to assail the astounded ears of unsuspecting and unprepared listeners in Ontario and Quebec. It must have been quite a shock as the melange of madness passed through these two provinces for the first time on its way to an already conditioned East Coast audience. Fairly recently I unearthed and listened to an old recording of that first ill-fated Rawhide program, and in retrospect I can now understand and fully sympathize with the ululations and beating of breasts that erupted the following day.

On that second day, with my first broadcast to a new audience under my belt, I came down to the studios around 7:45 a.m. to get the second onslaught ready. I was met in the basement corridor of the old Jarvis Street building by De B. Holley, who was just turning into one of the studios to read the 8:00 o'clock news.

"I'm awfully sorry about all this, Max. I hate to have to read it over the air, but it's one of the lead stories this morning and

I haven't any choice." These were the only words he tossed back at me over his shoulder before entering the studio and closing the door behind him.

Mystified, I wandered on down to the radio newsroom and asked what the trouble was. A gruff editor looked up from his typewriter long enough to grunt, "You!" and jerk his thumb in the direction of the closet-like room that housed all the teletype machines.

It was like reading my own epitaph as I watched dozens of unconcerned metal fingers dispassionately pounding out the words, "CBC announcer, Max Ferguson, who does a morning radio program in the guise of Old Rawhide, came in for a severe tongue-lashing yesterday on the floor of the House of Commons. Douglas Gooderham Ross, MP for the Toronto riding of St. Paul's, rose on the floor of the House to ask the speaker if he was aware of this program of meaningless ravings and tripe, disguised in the poorest possible English and an insult to the intelligence of thinking Canadians."

I was completely stunned — unable even to appreciate the wonderful irony of MPS being disturbed by poor English. I remember making my way in a daze upstairs to the announcers' lounge and slumping, limp and dejected, into a chair. I had been sitting alone brooding for possibly ten minutes when the phone rang and a huge, resonant voice asked for Max Ferguson. I identified myself suspiciously and asked who was speaking.

"This is Lorne Greene!" I fully expected a rundown on the day's news to follow, having heard that arresting opening line preceding the CBC news ever since I was in high school. I certainly wasn't prepared for what followed. "I've just read about you," the Golden Voice went on, "and your run-in with the House of Commons in the morning paper. My congratulations." I immediately took this as a piece of unsolicited sarcasm, and the hackles had just begun to rise on the back of my neck when the Voice went on, "Believe me, Max, you couldn't buy publicity like this for a million dollars. It won't do you a bit of harm. You're a lucky guy to get a break like this. All the best."

I mumbled my thanks and hung up the phone, which was still vibrating from the last vowel sound. Preposterous and all as his optimism appeared to be at the time, I was still amazed and gratified that he'd even bother to call a young neophyte in his blackest hour, and today every fist that Lorne gets in the mouth, every chair that's smashed over his head around the old Ponderosa, is like a lash across my own back.

Before the day was out, I was to learn that a St. Valentine's Day Massacre is just a word until you have one. Coupled with the MP's invective, a bucketful of hellfire and brimstone was also poured over my cowed head by a gentleman of the cloth in Ottawa, who volunteered in a press interview that my program was "a mixture of blasphemy and sacrilege that could only happen in Godless Soviet Russia." In the days that followed, the *Ottawa Citizen* devoted an entire page each day to its Letters to the Editor column to accommodate the overflow, pro and con, that resulted from the Rawhide controversy. There were, of course, small welcome shafts of sunlight that managed to filter down through the gathering storm clouds. One of these was a telegram sent to me from Ottawa by A. Davidson Dunton, then chairman of the CBC Board of Governors: "Having difficulty organizing support for campaign to make Rawhide mayor of Ottawa. Keep your fingers crossed and six-guns ready."

In Halifax, I was to learn later, students of Dalhousie University took over radio station CJCH for a "Defence of Rawhide" day. The Canadian Press carried on its wire service at the time an interview with Dr. Burns Martin, head of the English Department at Kings College in Halifax. He was a charmingly droll, white-haired old gentleman for whom I used to mark freshman English essays in my spare time during my Halifax days with the CBC. Asked to comment on the MP's indictment of Rawhide's English, he replied, "There was certainly no evidence of this shortcoming during the years he marked English essays at Kings College. If he has since acquired any bad habits in his use of the English language, they were undoubtedly picked up from some of the deplorable freshman English essays to which he was subjected."

Gradually, after two weeks of touch-and-go suspense, the tide began to turn in Rawhide's favour. Among the many letters that were still pouring in to both the CBC and the *Ottawa Citizen,* the "pros" began to outnumber the "cons". One of the last salvos fired by the retreating opposition was an absolute gem of a letter that appeared in the *Ottawa Citizen,* addressed to the editor. It was from an elderly retired army officer who couldn't have cared less what Rawhide said or how he said it. His complaint was of quite a different nature. Apparently for the past decade, his life had been so well ordered that he shaved each morning with meticulous military precision just as *Musical March Past* came on the air and was in the habit of matching the strokes of his straight razor with the lively martial theme that introduced the program. And so when 8:30 a.m. arrived on that black morning of February 14, the unfamiliar and erratic rhythm of *The Clarinet Polka* had completely fouled up his timing, and he was holding Rawhide and the CBC responsible for a badly lacerated face.

There was a most unusual and, for me, memorable denouement to this whole House of Commons affair. It began with a phone call late one evening at my home. On the other end of the line was the corporate voice of the CBC asking me to catch a plane to Ottawa first thing in the morning; the CBC thought it might be fun if Rawhide were to attend the Press Gallery Dinner to be held in Ottawa that evening. This annual dinner is quite an incredible event, rarely witnessed by laymen, at which the members of the press corps in Ottawa play host to the House of Commons and invited guests from the various embassies. It is an evening of light-hearted fun, during which the collective hair of all those attending is let down with one great thud, the reverberations of which fortunately never reach the newspapers, thanks to a gentlemen's agreement among the Fourth Estate. Since I had just survived two harrowing weeks which had left me with the disquieting impression that the entire House of Commons would like to see my dripping head nailed to the Peace Tower, I felt the CBC's insistence that I attend was an act of downright betrayal. Nevertheless, I obeyed, and by six o'clock the following evening Daniel was in the lions' den.

It was a large room somewhere in the Parliament Buildings, and the moment I entered it I stopped dead in my tracks. On one of the end walls hung a framed picture about five feet square. It was a dramatic and very formal photographic study of the then Prime Minister, the Rt. Hon. Louis St. Laurent. At least, the face was his. The body on which the head had been cut out and mounted was that of a convict wearing the traditional zebra suit. Underneath was the caption, "Louis the Lug". At the far end of the room, on the opposite end wall, an equally distinguished head of George Drew, leader of the opposition, gazed out impressively from the shoulders of a muscle-bound wrestler. Here the caption read simply, "Gorgeous George". In the ninety-foot area separating the two pictures, there were about two hundred noisy, boisterous male guests milling about with glasses, enjoying a quick few before the dinner that was shortly due to commence. The only person who knew of my presence there was the president of the Ottawa Press Gallery who, after meeting me earlier in the day, had brought me to the dinner and was now leading me, open-mouthed, across the room, where stood the only face familiar to me ... A. Davidson Dunton.

After a handshake and a friendly greeting, Dunton turned and led me a few steps away to where a rather large figure was standing with his back to us. When Dunton politely tapped on the broad shoulders, the figure turned around with a big, amiable grin, and I was introduced to George Drew. We had just begun to shake hands when a man pushed in between us, fixed George Drew with a slightly belligerent look and said, "I understand you weren't too happy with that profile I did on you in *Time* last week." Throughout this line Drew had continued pumping my hand as if he were expecting water. When the man finished his sentence, however, Drew dropped my hand, folded his fingers from the gesture of friendship into quite a formidable fist and directed it into the side of the man's face. A couple of bystanders restrained Drew from landing a second haymaker, while Dunton, suave and imperturbable as always, decided to see how far he'd get with a second introduction.

This one turned out to be one of the best-known cabinet ministers of the day. He was already moving across the room in our direction and was about five feet from us when Dunton finished shouting the introductions over the din of voices. The figure extended his hand and his face broke into a big, affable grin as he continued to advance toward us. Considering the aura of prestige which always surrounded this man's name, I'd love to be able to tell my grandchildren that I once shook his hand, but that was not to be. Unfortunately, he chose the wrong me from the double image that was obviously registering on his semi-anaesthetized retina. Missing my extended hand by a good foot, he continued on gamely with the smile still frozen on his face and the hand still out, until his momentum was rudely arrested by a very solid wall, which some builder years ago had carelessly left lying around. By this time bodies had begun sagging to the floor in crumpled heaps all over the room as if some phantom sniper were taking random shots. Two commissionaires were kept busy hauling away the casualties. I can truly say it was the wildest social evening I've ever attended in my life. Through it all, A. Davidson Dunton, the greatest public relations weapon the CBC ever had, stood matching them drink for drink and with not so much as a slurred consonant warded off a continuous barrage of charges and allegations against the CBC with his charming diplomacy and his masterfully vague replies.

Sometime later that evening, as I understood it, we were all summoned to dinner in another large room just off the one in which the cocktail hour had dragged on to such a disastrous finale. I found myself seated between the Italian ambassador and the ambassador from Northern Ireland. I can remember telling the latter with a loud laugh that all my relatives came from the "bomb-throwing" south of Ireland and was just warming up to my diplomatic icebreaker when a hand tapped me on the shoulder. It was the president of the Press Gallery whispering into my foggy left ear that he'd like a word with me just outside the doorway.

Once we were outside he hastily outlined the scenario of a

little leg-pulling jest which he felt would be fun to perpetrate on the assembled guests. My immediate role in the hoax was to conceal myself inside a type of collapsible cardboard wardrobe that had been set up just outside the doorway. I stepped in and the door closed behind me. The dark interior of my small cubicle was relieved by the light from one tiny crack, through which I could peer out and see about five feet of the head table. I noticed that a microphone had been placed inside with me. I could hear the steady buzz of dinner conversation and the rattle of plates and cutlery.

After standing in the semi-dark for what seemed like ages, I heard a burst of applause and then the voice of the Prime Minister. I was appalled to hear his brief speech interspersed with rude and rowdy interjections from the audience. "Aw come on, Louie, you gave us that old line last year!" "Hey, Louie — you don't expect us to swallow that guff do ya?" I listened with bated breath for the sharp staccato of a Mountie's side-arm, but there was none. This was apparently par for the course at Press Gallery dinners. Finally the president of the Press Gallery made his way to the microphone at the head table. In a believably serious voice he explained the efforts that had been made all week to arrange for Britain's illustrious Prime Minister, Winston Churchill, to be present at this function as guest of honour. (The old warrior was indeed visiting in New York at that very moment.) Due to his over-crowded itinerary, the speaker explained, such an appearance had proved to be out of the question; however, thanks to the kind co-operation of both the CBC and the Columbia Broadcasting System, the next best thing had been made possible. By direct line from New York the assembled guests were now going to hear a special message of greeting spoken by Mr. Churchill. Inside my murky cubicle I recognized this as the cue for which I had given up dinner. As the excited buzzing and restless stirring died down, I leaned into my microphone and sent booming into the room the best facsimile of Churchill's voice I could muster. You could hear a pin drop as the vocal hoax rolled out. As Churchill I spoke of the great pleasure it afforded me to know that my voice was reaching that distinguished gathering whose collective hand rested on the helm of the Canadian ship of state. I larded the speech with all the Churchillian expressions I could think of and concluded by citing and paying tribute to one or two Canadian public figures whom Churchill wished to thank for the assistance they had provided him in his mastery of the English language.... "Men such as your own Prime Minister, Loo-is Saynt Lor-ent, from whom I have learned much in the use of the Gallic idiom ... men such as your leader of the Canadian opposition, George Drew, from whom I've learned the power of invective. Yet, gentlemen, greater than any of these, as a teacher of that magnificent tongue which Shakespeare spake, is the man who at this moment stands by my side, the man whom I owe so much and on whom I now wish to call."

At this point I made an abrupt change into old Rawhide's voice and began to say, "Well, now, that's mighty nice of you to...." And that was as far as I got when the front of my hiding place suddenly pulled away and I was left standing, naked in my guilt before the entire multitude. There was an excruciating silence for about five full seconds. My gaze was pulled like a magnet to the steely look of Viscount Alexander, the then Governor-General, sitting at the centre of the head table. Twenty years seemed to drag by before he finally raised his hands and began to applaud. Mind you, it was not a hearty handclap. With the fingers of one hand he delicately patted the palm of the other as though he were packing an invisible pipe. It was, however, the official signal, the catalyst that drew from the entire room the most exciting ovation I've ever received.

While it was still ringing in my bewildered ears, three members of the press left their table and came running up to me. One of them shouted, "Tell Old Rawhide the only guy in the entire House of Commons we didn't invite here this evening was the one who lit into him on the floor of the House a couple of weeks ago!" Walking back to my room in the Chateau Laurier in the small and bitterly cold hours of that morning, I couldn't have wished for a more gratifying final chapter to the "House of Commons Affair".

From the beginning of the Toronto phase of the Rawhide program Marvin Mellobell, as director of the Rawhide Little Theatre group, was driven insatiably toward newer, more challenging, and more glorious horizons. His modest and unpretentious Halifax productions had been adequate, but he now found himself on the home ground of such titans in the field of radio drama as Andrew Allan and Esse W. Ljungh. With Marvin's formidable ego he looked upon these two as arch rivals in a triumvirate. He wasted no time in flinging open the doors of the world's great treasure-house of literature, grasping his players by the scruff of the neck and dragging them, unwilling and ill-equipped, to experience the dramatic delights that waited inside. Once inside, it must be admitted, the Rawhide Little Theatre Group seized upon those treasures with all the determination and finesse of a bulldog shaking a rat. *Hamlet, Macbeth, Romeo and Juliet, Julius Caesar, Wuthering Heights, Moby Dick, Treasure Island, The Scarlet Pimpernel, Dracula,* and *Frankenstein* — these and many others all went down like ninepins before the onslaught of the Group during those four Toronto-based years.

These were the only years in which I was forced to write legitimate scripts, albeit they were in pencilled longhand and, I'm sure, indecipherable to anyone but myself. In the earlier Halifax days, a few words hastily scribbled on the back of my cigarette package had sufficed, and in my current morning format dealing with the news stories that have just appeared a couple of hours prior to broadcast time, there just isn't time to write a word on paper.

In those Toronto years, 1949 to 1954, the Mellobell dramatic productions became so ambitious that I would often need about a dozen or more sound-effects records in a single fifteen-minute sketch. My poor operator didn't even have the luxury of a semi-legible script. After he was handed the pile of sound-effects records about ten minutes to air time, he was flying blind. It was essential, though, that I have some idea of where I was going in the sketch in order to be able to cue him in at the proper times. Under this catch-as-catch-can modus operandi, our rapport was often stretched to the breaking point and quite often we lost each other altogether.

One moment which would have been quite embarrassing on any other program but Rawhide's was the occasion when the Little Theatre Group offered *The Phantom of the Opera*. The Phantom, played by the raucous-voiced Arnprior character, was busily sawing away at the huge chandelier that hung in the dome of the Paris Opera House over the heads of the terrified audience. While I desperately tried to indicate to my operator through the control-room glass that I wanted the sound of the chandelier crashing, I stalled for time by having the Phantom hurl down such dramatic inspirations as, "Boy, are youse guys down there ever gonna get it! Yessir, boy, I'm really gonna fix you good ... in a coupla minutes." Finally the operator launched the long-awaited sound-effect record on the turntable, and the next thing the audience along the network heard was a completely incongruous staccato burst of machine-gun fire, followed by the Phantom's voice yelling, "And if there's any CBC operators down there among youse opera lovers, that there's just a small example of what they're gonna get if this here chandelier don't come down pretty soon!"

Quite often a script would call for a sound effect that wasn't available among the records in the CBC sound-effects library. At such times I would try to improvise as best I could in the studio with manual sound. *The Scarlet Pimpernel* was a good example. Five minutes to air time I still had no idea of how I was going to simulate the all-important sound of the guillotine. I ended up racing down the studio hallway to the radio newsroom, hastily commandeering a large, heavy swivel chair mounted on wheels and dragging it back to my little studio just in time to open my mike switch and start the program. Whenever I needed the guillotine, I would cue my operator for a recorded drum roll and the second this finished I would shove the big chair as hard as I could across the studio floor and into the far wall. It worked beautifully, with the squeaky, rattling wheels suggesting rope spinning through a rusty pulley. When the chair crashed into the studio wall, the final arrest of the guillotine blade, I cued again for the recorded cheering and laughter of old crones.

The day following this last-minute improvisation, a memo was slipped into my mail slot in the announcers' lounge. It was addressed to Marvin Mellobell and read, "For years I've longed to do Pimpernel on the CBC Stage Series, but the sound of the guillotine has always frustrated me. In view of the brilliant and effective way you overcame the problem yesterday, I have no other choice but to resign forthwith as Supervisor of Radio Drama for the CBC and name you my successor." It was signed, Andrew Allan.

I've always been intrigued by the unlimited potential of sound effects in radio and the wonderfully believable illusions that can be created with them. No matter how wildly I departed from the original intent of an author, no matter what licence I took with his immortal lines, I always strove to make my sound as authentic as possible. Somehow the believability of the sound seemed to heighten the nonsense of the dialogue. In Marvin's presentation of *Treasure Island*, for example, my operator rose to the occasion with a marvellously realistic background of creaking timbers, crashing waves, howling winds, and a dozen other shipboard effects recalling the great days of sail. The crew, outward-bound from Portsmouth, had been at sea for weeks, beleaguered by dense fog all the way. Finally it began to lift, and a great cheer went up from all hands at the prospect of seeing at last their long-awaited Treasure Island. It turned out, of course, that they were still in Portsmouth Harbour, having overlooked the bothersome detail of hauling anchor. The captain bellowed a mighty and exasperated "Avast!", a crew-member meekly enquired, "Avast what?", and the captain replied, "Avast ya a thousand times to weigh that bloomin' anchor afore we sailed anywhere!" Then in came the *Clarinet Polka* and mercifully washed out another Marvin Mellobell production.

As the Rawhide program finished each morning at 9:00 o'clock Toronto time, my day as a CBC staff announcer would be just beginning. This, after all, was the job for which I was being paid by the CBC and the Rawhide program, for the eight years I was on CBC staff, was done without any remuneration simply because I enjoyed doing it and it provided a pleasant counterbalance to my more prosaic and less challenging announce duties. Even before the Rawhide program came on the air at 8:30 each morning, I would often be assigned to the program *Morning Devotions* as the duty announcer. This meant that after introducing the guest minister and dozing lightly through the ensuing fifteen minutes, I would have to sign him off, deliver the CBC cue, and then be in my own studio one floor below, ready to begin as Rawhide. I had exactly twenty seconds in which to exit from the *Morning Devotions* studio, sprint down a hall, fly down two flights of stairs, execute a speedy fifty-yard dash to the Rawhide studio, and still have enough wind left to do the slow, relaxed drawl of old Rawhide.

One morning while the guest minister and I sat facing each other across the microphone, waiting for Morning Devotions to begin and making polite, general conversation, he suddenly asked me if I knew "this dreadful Rawhide character." I replied evasively that I had seen him around on occasion. He then began to fill the remaining few minutes to broadcast time with a spirited account of what he'd say to this wretch if he should ever run across him. What particularly bothered him was that one of his congregation, an English lady sent out to Canada by her doctor for reasons of health, was up every morning listening to Rawhide instead of getting extra sleep. I agreed that all this was a shocking state of affairs and that, really, something should be done about Rawhide.

With the arrival of airtime, he was forced to supplant his venomous views on Rawhide with fifteen minutes of sweetness and light directed to the listening audience. But immediately after I signed off the program and was preparing for my mad dash downstairs, he got back to the subject of Rawhide again. This time he asked me where the offensive program was perpetrated each morning. With precious seconds ticking by, I replied as vaguely as I could that it was done somewhere downstairs. Then, inventing the excuse that I had left my car in a no-parking zone on Jarvis Street, I gave him a warm Christian handshake and raced like the wind.

My Rawhide theme was already playing when I burst into the little studio downstairs, settled into my chair before the microphone, and began the usual facial contortions that always accompanied my slipping from Dr. Jekyll into Mr. (Raw) Hyde. When I heard the theme fading down, I began in Rawhide's voice, "Well howdy! This is old Rawhide bustin' out of CBC Toronto just in time to ruin that second cup of coffee for you which you shouldn't be drinking anyway if you're a decent, conscientious mother and have any intention of getting those poor little neglected kids off to school." At this point something extra-sensory made me look up, and there in the control room, peering through the glass at me over a stiff, clerical collar, was the very red and very bewildered face of my friend who, brief moments ago, had shared a common bond with me in our mutual loathing and hearty disapproval of Rawhide. I continued ad-libbing my opening remarks and followed him with a friendly smile as he slowly backed out of the control room ... a visibly shaken man.

Looking back over my eight lacklustre years spent as a CBC staff announcer, there is really only one distinction I can claim. As Rawhide always said whenever he introduced a certain English counter-tenor, some people are cut out for their professions. I was never cut out to be an announcer. The only accolade to which I lay claim is the fact that no announcer in Canadian radio has ever equalled, or can hope to equal, the one and only Royal Tour broadcast to which I was assigned in the early fifties. For drabness, flatness, and dullness it stands alone in the entire history of Royal Tour broadcasting — a colossal, monumental dud that resulted in my being relieved of all other Royal Tour assignments that had been entrusted to me.

At three o'clock on the day which was to have been my finest hour, I was stationed at my Royal Tour observation post high atop the roof of the Automotive Building at the CNE grounds. With me was my "co-observer", Bob Brazil, sent up for the occasion from the CBC announce staff in Montreal. There were also bodies scattered about on various rooftops all over downtown Toronto, including the BBC's veteran and highly competent expert on outside broadcasting, John Snagg.

A master control point had been set up from which the co-ordinating producer, Reid Forsee, could mastermind the whole broadcast like a chess player with his pawns. Through the earphones which all of us were wearing we could be given the cue to start our commentary as soon as the royal entourage approached our position. Another cue would then be given to wrap it up and turn it over to the next observer once the Royal motorcade had passed one position and was approaching the next.

At our location, Bob Brazil and I found one solitary microphone waiting for us — a breast-plate type that had to be wriggled into, then the umpteen straps adjusted, tightened, and fastened so that the microphone came to rest snugly on the chest just flush with the mouth. It required only about fifteen minutes of wrestling before one could slip into it with approximately the same ease as a medieval chastity belt, I would imagine. Bob, an ex-Mountie who stood about six feet, seven inches, and who, when he'd worked on the CBC Halifax announce staff with me, had earned the nickname "B'ar Hug", kindly offered to let me climb into it first. Our view commanded Lake Ontario, a stretch of Lakeshore Boulevard leading to the Humber Bridge, and for good measure, a young couple of star-crossed lovers disconcertingly sprawled on the grass fifty feet below us where, Royal Tours notwithstanding, they were endeavouring to "make the beast with the double back".

We were to be the first on the air that afternoon, since the Royal Motorcade, coming in from Malton Airport, would enter Toronto from the west and pass over the Humber Bridge. At about half-past three I heard the voice of our co-ordinating producer crackling into my earphones. "We've just got word they'll be coming over the Humber Bridge in a few minutes, Max. You're on in ten seconds ... five seconds, three, two, one ... take it!"

I began by informing a breathlessly awaiting nation that their Highnesses would be along at any moment. Then I launched into a brief description of the scene before me — hundreds of people lining Lakeshore Boulevard, the blue

74

dancing waters of Lake Ontario, and the lovely lawns of the C.N.E. buildings. I was careful to avoid that small patch of uninhibited passion immediately below me which had now become pretty well flattened. Ten minutes stretched into fifteen, fifteen into half an hour, until finally I had been babbling on for one entire hour without a sign of the Royal motorcade. In my ears constantly was the disconcerting voice of the producer, muttering half to himself and half to me that he just couldn't understand what had become of the Royal couple. This distraction in my earphones was just about all I needed at that point, because the ad-libs were getting increasingly feeble as it was. "Don't try to push it, Max," the voice went on, "turn it over to Bob Brazil."

By now I was so desperate for things to talk about that I seriously entertained the idea of letting the network audience in on the endeavours of the Kinsey Kids on the grass below. However, a quick downward glance ruled out even this indiscreet possibility; the pair had apparently grown tired of waiting for their Queen and, having neither the energy or imagination to devise a new method of killing time, had departed.

"Max, did you hear me? Don't kill yourself ... turn the mike over to Bob Brazil!"

What the producer didn't know and what I couldn't tell him was that I was strapped into a breast-plate mike that would take about fifteen minutes to wriggle out of and then re-adjust to accommodate the gargantuan frame of Bob Brazil. I plodded on, describing the lengthening shadows of the trees and buildings, the chilly breeze coming in off Lake Ontario. Then, like a drowning man spotting a straw, I noticed two little ducks about a hundred yards out in the lake bobbing up and down in the swell. They were ordinary, drab, run-of-the-mill, brown ducks, but in my mounting panic they became "little feathered subjects perhaps only dimly aware of the great spectacle soon to unfold and already waiting to pay silent homage to Her Majesty."

This occasioned a fresh and even more frantic crackling in my earphones. "For God's sake, Max, turn it over to Bob Brazil! Don't strain! Something's gone wrong! Nobody knows when they're coming. *Give it to Bob!"*

At the end of my patience and linguistic rope, I decided then and there that since I couldn't "Give it to Bob", I'd give it to my poor producer instead. "Ladies and gentlemen," I confided to the network audience, "I'm going to have to take you for a moment behind the scenes of the fascinating world we call radio and let you in on one of those little moments of crisis that are sent to try men's souls. I am being asked repeatedly in my earphones, by a producer several miles away, to hand the microphone over to my co-observer. What my producer apparently doesn't realize (here my voice built to a loud shout hurled into the mike from a sixteenth of an inch away) is that I'm *strapped inextricably into a* BREAST-PLATE MIKE!" Allowing a moment for this information to sink in, I then resumed the commentary, assuming that I had at last rid myself of this terribly disconcerting voice in my ear.

I think I was in the middle of counting the number of lamp standards along Lakeshore Boulevard when the apology arrived. "Max, I'm terribly sorry, fella," the catharsis began, "I had no idea you were wearing a breastplate mike. Naturally you couldn't possibly turn it over to Bob. Gee, I should have known you had a problem there. I'm awfully sorry, really I am ..." and so on until, without waiting for permission, I finally flung the broadcast, like a rotten fish, over to the next broadcast position along the route.

It was seven o'clock that evening when the Royal motorcade finally appeared at the Humber Bridge and I got my cue to come on the air again for the real thing. By this time it was quite dark, bitterly cold, and the last of the crowds had lumped off home with their little Union Jacks still clutched in their frozen fists. I explained the dismal, deserted scene to the listening audience and then confessed that although five or six cars were, at present, driving past, it was impossible to tell which one was the Royal car. Strangely enough, it turned out that at the very moment I said those words Prince Philip, who had been listening on the car radio to the whole debacle, had asked the driver to blink the car lights as a signal. Looking back on it, I can only conclude that the chauffeur must have pulled the Royal cigarette lighter in and out, or perhaps the Royal windshield wipers, because I certainly didn't see any blinking lights.

The only thing I saw was a flash of light as a photographer snapped the picture of a small boy, the only human being there to witness the passing of their Royal Highnesses. He was all alone, standing against a lamp standard waving his little flag like a wound-up mechanical toy. I devoted the remaining moments of my commentary to the young lad, explaining to the audience that his picture would probably be appearing in the newspapers the next day with a poignant, heart-rending story of how the plucky little fellow had braved the elements to greet his Queen. Then, like a wet blanket, I advised them not to believe a word of it. I had watched the little chap arriving in a nice warm car just about five minutes before the Royal motorcade came by. He had been taken by the hand and propped by the photographer against the lamp standard. Unlike the hundreds of little kids who had waited for four hours before being taken home and put to bed, this little commercial plant had suffered no inconvenience whatever. I was to learn the next day that I'd incurred the undying wrath of a well-known Toronto commercial photographer, who had planned to sell this poignant little money-maker to the press but had been turned down thanks to my big cynical mouth.

Later that evening, after we all slithered down off our respective rooftops, we reported back to the CBC board room for a strategy planning meeting in preparation for the further Royal Tour Olympic heights we were going to scale in the next few days. The most strategic decision to come out of that meeting was the one to relieve me of my remaining Royal Tour assignments.

Some of my more pleasant memories of the straight announcing duties I performed for the CBC in Toronto were those occasions on a Wednesday evening when I found myself assigned to James Bannerman's Introduction to CBC *Wednesday Night*. Long before I'd ever met Bannerman I had made him, through mimicry, a fairly frequent visitor to the Rawhide show. Considering the man's intellect, erudition, and prestigious position in CBC programming, he had every right to be furious at the outrageous nonsense I put into his mouth on such occasions. During one of Marvin Mellobell's reports, for example, from a large Toronto department store one Christmas when he described the wide variety of toys available to shoppers, Bannerman turned up on the doll counter —a living, breathing Chatty Bannerman doll waiting to delight some tot on Christmas morning. When Marvin accepted the clerk's invitation to pull out the small ring in Bannerman's back, that distinctive voice, symbolic of all that's best in CBC radio, was heard with the plaintive appeal, "This is CBC *Wednesday Night* ... please put me to bed." For about four consecutive years in Marvin's ill-fated commentary on the gigantic parade which annually heralds Santa's arrival in Toronto, the CBC float was supposed to be the highlight of the parade. It was a huge, electronically activated effigy of James Bannerman. Under about a ton of paper-mache, the collective genius of CBC engineering minds had installed a complicated mass of electronic circuitry that was intended to make the figure both move and speak. Each year it was patiently entered in the hope of overshadowing old Santa himself and at the same time, getting in a dramatic plug for CBC *Wednesday Night.* Ideally the figure, which the CBC always stuck strategically in front of Santa's own float, would slowly turn its head from side to side, make waving gestures to the thousands of delighted children, and speak the characteristic line, "Good evening. This is James Bannerman!"

But it never quite happened that way. Invariably each year, as the float approached Marvin's broadcast position, his voice would mount hysterically with an effusion of CBC loyalty and pride as he prepared his audience for the CBC's finest hour. Then suddenly there would be a series of small backfirings and sputterings, and Marvin, in a voice choked with horror and dismay, would be forced to describe the three CBC engineers armed with wrenches and screwdrivers who at that moment were running alongside the float, desperately attempting to correct their faulty wiring. All the while, the voice of the effigy would be heard in the background mouthing its garbled line, "Is ... James ... Bannerman ... good ... this ... evening?" with a malicious inflection which obviously was inviting a negative reply.

Bannerman's reaction to these repeated and impudent affronts to his dignity was to either phone immediately or write me a letter expressing the most enthusiastic and jovial appreciation. It always amazes me when someone occasionally asks, "What's this Bannerman like ... kind of stuffy?" I invariably answer by recounting what I know of the man's incredible background — a professional boxer, naval officer, race car driver, a guide cum gigolo available for hire by wealthy ladies who wished to see Europe, a man who can guess your weight to the pound, having learned the art while living and travelling with gypsies, and undoubtedly, a man who somewhere along the line has managed to amass a formidable knowledge of the world around him.

Bannerman, to my way of thinking, embodies the most fascinating blend of the scholarly academic and the earthy stevedore. His coherent and always stimulating speech is a remarkable mixture of Conrad and Rabelais. I well remember putting him on the air one evening out of the little cubicle called Studio J from which he originated his introductions to CBC *Wednesday Night.* The feature broadcast that evening was devoted to the work of a well-renowned contemporary English poet. Bannerman used his fifteen minutes of program time to discuss the man and his poetry. I remember sitting across the microphone from him, listening absolutely enthralled by his eloquently expressed and brilliantly researched material. When he finished the broadcast I signed him off and gave the Corporation cue. We both then headed for the studio door, and I couldn't refrain from complimenting him on a most scholarly performance. He thanked me with obvious embarrassment and then confided, "I'm afraid it was a bit long-winded but unfortunately, in CBC *Wednesday Night* language, it takes fifteen minutes of euphemism to say that the son of a bitch would have been a much better poet if his testicles had only descended." If I were to read volumes of biographic study on this "stuffy" personality, this is still *the* line by which I'll always remember James Bannerman.

Just as colourful and irrepressible as any of my imaginary Rawhide characters was a CBC staff employee who used to visit the program once each year in the flesh and not through the device of mimicry. Eddie Dunne, Ireland's wonderful gift to the CBC, came originally from Cork and looked like Victor McLaglen compressed into about five feet, two inches. Eddie was a maintenance man around the studios, and I usually encountered him with a ladder under his arm on his way to replace a defective light bulb or a broken window. He had caches of beer hidden in strategic, secret locations all through the premises of 354 Jarvis Street. The hard liquor, however, was confined to one central hiding place — a glorified broom closet situated at the end of the long downstairs studio corridor. This was where Eddie held court in his spare time, divulging to an enrapt coterie of announcers, engineers, and junior producers top management program and policy secrets weeks before they were officially announced. His reputation as the Delphic oracle of the CBC was such that on one occasion, when a CBC executive had been missing on supposed CBC business in Europe for several weeks, a contingent of top management marched in one day to confront Eddie in the little broom-cluttered salon and ask him if he knew where the A.W.O.L. culprit was. Eddie led them to a wall on which he had thumb-tacked quite an exotic collection of postcards sent to him from far-flung corners of Europe by the miscreant and each bearing the usual cliché about having a wonderful time. Judging from the semi-legible scrawl, such a piece of information seemed quite superfluous. Thanks to this telltale postal paper chase, the sleuths were able at least to discover that the last known whereabouts of their wandering boy was the Vatican. Eddie's conversation was difficult to follow, as the thick Cork accent had to fight its way out through a nose that had been broken in several places, but it was magnificently larded with natural Irish wit. The tough little kids who shared the fashionable Jarvis Street neighbourhood with the CBC and whom Eddie

AND NOW ... HERE'S MAX

often had to chase out of the building were always referred to by him as "brothel sprouts". He also had wonderful stories about the Irish wakes he'd been to right in the heart of Toronto. At one of these, he told us, the corpse had been removed from the casket in order to accommodate one of the mourners, who wanted to lie down for just a few minutes and ended up stretched out in the satin for three solid days.

It became a sort of tradition that Eddie would drop in as Rawhide's only live, flesh-and-blood guest every St. Patrick's Day morning. Since he always took what he called "a running start" at St. Patrick's Day, getting into the festive cup at about eight the previous evening, Eddie was always "delivered" to the studio each St. Patrick's Day morning by friends. After one or two Irish records, Rawhide would introduce Eddie and interview him about Ireland. No matter how assiduously Rawhide tried to introduce such topics as leprechauns, shamrock, and other innocuous bits of Irish culture Eddie would always get onto the Black and Tans and would have to be washed out with a recording just as the profanity started.

One year, just after we had concluded the St. Patrick's Day edition of the Rawhide show, Eddie insisted we repair to the broom closet at the end of the hall and drink a toast to Ireland. Over a bottle of Bushmills' Irish Whiskey he asked me how I felt he had done on the air. I told him I thought he'd done very well, but there was something bothering him, and he wouldn't accept my assurance that it had been a good performance. He was upset that he had completely forgotten to tell the audience how shillelaghs are made. He told me that he'd been up all night riding the TTC all over Toronto and preparing a little treatise on the making of shillelaghs. Somehow, in the course of the broadcast, possibly due to nervous tension, the whole thing had gone out of his mind. He kept insisting that he'd let me down and also the audience. Eventually, he had me agreeing with him that it was a darn shame that he'd forgotten this little talk that would have been so interesting to the network audience. After fifteen minutes of mutual and maudlin lamenting over what Canadian radio had just missed, I innocently asked how shillelaghs *were* made and

81

learned to my horror how close my career had come to ending. "Dey makes 'em," said Eddie in the most ingenuous voice, "out of a bull's penis."

V

ALL THE EDDIE Dunnes — the characters, the eccentrics, the clowns —who lent such a wonderfully stimulating wackiness to the CBC daily routine a decade ago have pretty well vanished from the scene now. Today the pace is comfortably routine, spiritlessly methodical, and reasonably efficient. For one thing, the Moon Radiant hasn't been around for years. It was generally on Saturday mornings he used to wander in off Jarvis Street, draped in a loose-fitting, white, toga-like garment. With long, sandy hair falling loosely to his shoulders, he bore a disturbing resemblance to Christ, even when he stood munching on a piece of raw meat. His mission was always the same. He would march up to the reception desk in the CBC lobby and demand to see the general manager concerning all the accumulated royalties owed him by the CBC. Since he had discovered electricity on the moon some years previously, the CBC had been stealing it for broadcast purposes and now owed him a staggering sum for this bootlegged utility. With the studied and efficient charm of an Air Canada stewardess, the CBC receptionist would fob him off on each occasion by saying that the CBC general manager was, unfortunately, not on the premises.

One morning just as he was being repulsed by the receptionist, announcer De B. Holly and I decided to lend him a helping hand. He was backing away from the reception desk, thanking the girl for her kindness and promising to send her a tiara of moon gems for her trouble, when we stepped forward and asked him would he settle for the CBC Director of Personnel and Administration. When he said he would, we directed him across the lobby to the office of Mr. Van Bommel who was, in fact, Director of Personnel and Administration and who had popped into his office in the hope of getting some work cleared up during the quiet of a Saturday morning

83

when there was no staff around to bother him.

As the Moon Radiant swept in through his office door, De B. and I lurked behind in the outer office, where we could both watch and hear what went on without Van Bommel's seeing us. I must admit that in spite of the inner tension that must have gripped him when he saw such a strange apparition coming through his office door, Van Bommel played it very cool on the outside. He stood and offered the Moon Radiant a chair. Then, asking what he could do for his guest, he settled back with his arms folded across his chest and listened while the latter unfolded the tale of the CBC's illegal use of his moon electricity. Van Bommel promised to look into it, then rose smiling as if to suggest that, although the visit had been charming, he now had other things he'd like to get done.

The Moon Radiant, however, having established this much of a toehold, was not settling for any more bum's rushes from the CBC no matter how charmingly they were brought off. As we peered through the slightly open door of the outer office, De B. and I could see Van Bommel subsiding into his chair while the Moon Radiant demanded to know why the CBC was not broadcasting in moon language to the people of Canada. There was only a momentary moistening of the lips before Van Bommel had the answer to that one. Heavens, there was nothing the CBC would like better than to be able to broadcast in moon language to the people of Canada. It was a great idea, and the CBC was all for it, except that the people of Canada didn't *know* moon language. From our vantage point we watched the effulgent glow of satisfaction that broke over Van Bommel's face as he tossed that impromptu and divinely inspired piece of irrefutable logic at the Moon Radiant.

But the Moon Radiant wasn't finished yet. Reaching into the loose folds of his garment, he pulled out a little notebook which he thrust at Van Bommel. It was, he explained, a concise English-Moon pocket dictionary that he had compiled and that the CBC could easily have printed and sent out to every home in Canada. Van Bommel's sangfroid showed the first signs of disintegrating as he sat desperately staring at the scribbled gibberish in the little notebook, chewing nervously on his bottom lip.

It was then that Holly delivered the coup de grace. Picking up the phone in front of him, he dialled Van Bommel's local. We heard the phone ring and could also see Van Bommel picking it up. "Mr. Van Bommel," said Holly, lowering his voice to make it both authoritative and ominous, "that man sitting across from you has pronounced homicidal tendencies. There's a long butcher knife concealed under his robes. As long as you don't antagonize him, I think you'll be alright. I'm going out for reinforcements." We left almost immediately then, since we both had program deadlines to make in other parts of the building, and the last we saw of Van Bommel was a pallid face bravely trying to muster up a weak, mechanical smile as he replaced the phone like a drowning man giving up his straw and sat stiffly facing the Moon Radiant to begin what must have been a long wait for reinforcements.

There was another character, back in the early fifties, whom a lot of CBC Toronto staff knew about but had never seen. She was the dear old lady, Mrs. J.A.D. Montgomery, who used to phone announcer Ken Murray every morning immediately after he had finished his hour-long program of classical music, *Music In the Morning*. Many's the morning I would walk into CJBC studio and sit for fully thirty minutes listening to Ken Murray desperately trying to get away from the phone without hurting the poor old soul's feelings. Sometimes during a particularly long profusion of eulogy which didn't require any response from Ken, he would hand the phone over to me and I'd listen. It was a tiny, thin, quavering voice on the other end, and generally it rattled off the many rewards which God would unquestionably bestow upon Ken in the hereafter for all the enjoyment he had brought to listeners over the years through his delightful program. When at last Ken would manage to hang up and extricate himself from the smothering profusion of accolades which had been showered upon him, he would make some feeble protest of annoyance that was never quite strong enough to disguise the fact that he was really quite delighted that any listener would think enough of him to phone each morning with such extravagant praise.

One morning after this telephone tryst had been going on with unremitting regularity for almost a year, I walked out of CJBC studio where Ken was still modestly declining the laurel wreath that the dear old soul had chosen to place on his brow that morning. Realizing Ken would be tied up for some time, I walked the few steps down the hall to visit De B. Holly, who was on duty in the adjacent CBL Studio. When I opened the studio door and walked in, De B. was on the phone, and the first words I heard, spoken in a tiny, thin, quavering voice were "No, no, no, Mr. Murray, you're altogether too modest. You are *not* just doing your CBC job. This great joy which you bring to the hearts of thousands each morning with your glorious music is certainly being recorded in the Golden Book and I'm quite certain that when our Heavenly Father calls us all home at the end of life's troubled ... etc., etc."

After a year of making her calls in secret, the "dear old soul" was a bit disconcerted to find an interloper standing over her, arms folded, casting a reproachful glance in her direction. She rang off with a hasty, "God bless you Mr. Murray. I must go now." De B. swore me to secrecy and then divulged his long-range plan for Ken Murray. All these phoney morning phone calls, painstakingly made over the period of a year, were intended merely as a softening-up process in preparation for the master stroke. In about a week's time, when the ring had been securely fitted through Ken Murray's nose, the dear old soul was going to invite him to meet her for dinner in the Imperial Dining Room of the Royal York Hotel. After coming halfway across Toronto for the rendezvous, Ken would then be left sitting, like Keats' still-unravished bride of quiet time, for an old lady who would never turn up. I should like to believe it was Christian charity which made De B. ultimately forego his plans, but I suspect it was his having to divulge the scheme to me which unnerved him. At any rate, Ken Murray received no further calls from sweet old Mrs. J.A.D. Montgomery and to this day believes she either died or moved away. Considerably more corporeal than the mythical Mrs. J.A.D. Montgomery was the mammoth old Scottish charwoman who used to clean up around the studios every evening some years ago. Her itinerary with scrub brush and pail was very precise. At ten o'clock each evening she would start on her hands and knees down the long studio corridor, scrubbing with powerful strokes of her huge forearms as if her life depended on erasing every trace of pattern from the CBC linoleum. I would always be sitting in CBL studio at the far end of the hallway, feverishly rolling cigarettes with my five-at-one-blow V-Master. At a few minutes to eleven I would hear the faint rattling of the pail and the sound of the scrub brush approaching. Then in another few minutes there would come a tapping behind me on the glass window, and I would turn to see two beady eyes peering in over the sill. As the sill was only three feet off the floor, one got the impression of being watched by a tiny dwarf or even a raven until, of course, one realized that like an iceberg four-fifths of that massive bulk was out of sight, supported on its hands and knees. There would be a few interrogative gyrations of the eyebrows, which in a woman of younger years would have been quite indecent, but which in her case were simply a sort of char semaphore asking was it alright to come in and clean CBL studio. I would always smile and nod my head to indicate that I wasn't on the air and that the coast was clear. The door would then open and in she'd come, advancing at incredible speed on her hands and knees toward me so that she ended up with her nose just touching the long surface of the microphone table on which was spread the entire affluent harvest of six hours steady rolling, about two hundred cigarettes.

The opening gambit was always the same, delivered with the same disarming and innocuous candour. "Would ye hae a cigarette to spare, laddie?" It got to be a completely rhetorical question because, without waiting for my answer, she would immediately delve into the folds of her dress and produce a large brown paper bag of the type usually used for carrying home a weekend's groceries. This would be held open at the end of the table while a gigantic Popeye forearm would reach out and sweep about four square feet of table, so that at least three hours of painstaking rolling would go cascading off the end of the table and into the gaping maw of the brown paper bag she always just seemed to have with her. I suppose I could have hidden all those cigarettes when the first pail-rattling drifted down the hallway or, even after she asked, flung myself spread-eagle on top of the lot screaming hysterically, "No, you can't ... you can't ... they're mine ... all mine!" I feel quite sure I could have done this if only she'd come in standing up. But what would have been pure and easily resisted scrounging in an upright position suddenly became poignant and heart-rending supplication when she resorted to the hands and knees technique, and so the massive, nocturnal purloining went on without remission for months.

The old CBC canteen down in the bowels of the radio building at 354 Jarvis Street is a rather quiet and lacklustre place these days. I still pop in for coffee after my program each morning, but it's not the adventure it used to be. I miss the booming baritone voice of folk singer Ed McCurdy. He used to sit in a corner filing his nails while he filled the canteen with his magnificent voice. The melodies were usually esoteric Elizabethan airs and the lyrics were always filthy. Generally, he directed his unsolicited serenade toward a table of young CBC secretaries, who would abandon half-drunk cups of coffee and rush crimson-faced back to the sanctuary of their offices. The ditties are no longer heard around the CBC canteen, but in all probability they waft now and again through the regal chambers of Buckingham Palace. When McCurdy later drew from his gamey repertoire and made an LP called *When Dalliance Was In Flower,* one of the first buyers was His Royal Highness Prince Philip. I often wonder if Her Majesty's morning coffee is periodically ruined, or whether, perhaps, she's made of sterner stuff than CBC secretaries.

I used to see quite a bit of Murray Westgate in the canteen in the early fifties. Murray had just arrived from the West Coast to try his hand at the acting game in Toronto. This would have been a few years before Imperial Oil turned him into the best-known service station operator in the country, and in those days, with acting jobs not too plentiful, Murray had lots of spare time to sit over a coffee and

AND NOW ... HERE'S MAX

regale us with some wonderful stories of his earlier attempts
to earn a living on the West Coast. At one stage he had
worked for some sort of travelling show. While the regular
shill stood out in front extolling the merits of a revolution-
ary new orange squeezer, Murray's job was to sit in the back
of the tent and inject buckets of artificial orange juice into
the oranges which the shill was going to use in his demonstration of the remarkable new squeezer. First, of course, the
shill would demonstrate the mediocre results obtained by
using an ordinary squeezer. Then selecting one of Murray's
artificially bloated oranges, he would demonstrate the new
squeezer with startling success. The job abruptly terminated
for Murray the day he got two groups of oranges mixed up
and the shill, after disdainfully dismissing the old fashioned
squeezer as a hopelessly inefficient time-waster, pressed
the wrong orange onto it and was immediately engulfed in a
veritable tidal wave of orange juice.

The year of the Toronto TTC strike I remember en-
countering in the canteen one day a visibly shaken and
upset Austin Willis. He explained how he had started off
for the studios that day hitch-hiking, like most Torontonians who found themselves caught without any form of
public transportation. Somewhere along Bay Street a most
opulent-looking elderly gentleman pulled up and beckoned
him into his very sleek and expensive car. As they drove
along, the tycoon divulged to Austin that he was normally
wary of strangers, especially the type of uncouth ruffians
which were to be seen loitering about the street corners of
Toronto. Never in his life had he stopped to offer a lift to
anyone. However, he went on, he was so impressed with
Austin's unusually distinguished and aristocratic bearing that
he had decided to risk offering him a ride, and, indeed,
he hadn't regretted it. He was delighted with Austin's
ability to converse with such polished urbanity. As Austin indicated that the next traffic light would be as far as
he wished to go, the old gentleman continued his rhapsodic
tribute, saying it wasn't very often in this day and age that
one was fortunate enough to encounter a thorough and

well-spoken gentleman. When the car eased to a stop at the red light, Austin thanked him for his kindness, but the old chap insisted it had been his pleasure. The brief few minutes of their chance encounter had been most delightful. Austin then stepped out into the winter slush at the corner of Bay and Wellesley and slammed the car door shut. Just as the light turned green and the limousine began to slowly pull away, Austin noticed a man's rubber lying in the slush of the road where it had fallen, he assumed, when the car door had opened. The car was now well out into the intersection and Austin realized the only chance he had of returning the lost article to his benefactor was to pitch it underhand through the half-open window on the passenger side.

He ran a few steps until he was almost abreast of the window. Then he pitched the rubber, which sailed in through the window alright, but then kept on going till it hit the old gentleman a soggy whack on the side of his well-groomed head. As the car continued on, Austin observed the flushed face looking back over its shoulder in wide-eyed incredulity. Then he looked down to find that one of his own rubbers was missing. The only conclusion he could possibly have left with the old gentleman was that his urbane and aristocratic hitch-hiker, after accepting the old boy's generosity and compliments, had callously pulled off one of his rubbers upon alighting and for no reason whatsoever lobbed it at him in return for favours received.

I wonder whatever became of the little chap who joined the CBC night cleaning staff a few years ago? He lasted only a couple of nights, but in that short time managed to cover himself with sufficient glory to ensure that his memory will live on as long as CBC sagas continue to be swapped over cups of morning coffee. Before embarking on his cleaning duties around the radio building, he was given a thorough indoctrination lecture by his cleaning boss on the fine old CBC tradition of thoroughness and efficiency. There was to be no shirking of duty. Every inch of that CBC radio building was to be cleaned, waxed, and polished. Although as a recent immigrant he was new to the ways of Canada and the CBC, and although he didn't understand all the words spoken to him, a good bit of the pep talk must have struck home, because off he went with his cloth, wax, and polisher down the linoleum of the lower studio corridor, working like a Trojan. Not a square foot of floor escaped the diligent and conscientious application of great dollops of paste wax and the whirring brushes of the polisher, not even the broadloom in the night manager's office. Its knotted and coagulated pile, in spite of the most ingenious restorative attempts by a competent Toronto dry cleaner, never did snap back to the opulent status symbol it once had been.

It would be inaccurate to give the impression that the CBC of yesteryear was always light-hearted and gay. There were some moments of tragedy and disaster. In the summer of 1952 the operator of the CBC canteen (one in a long list of ill-fated entrepreneurs who failed to realize just how long CBC types can dawdle over a ten-cent cup of coffee) was a man by the name of Bert Pooler. Bert used to stand all day beside his cash register, a cigar in his mouth and a look of far-off horizons in his rather baleful, owlish eyes. We always knew that he was daydreaming about his stocks. It was common knowledge that Bert played the stock market quite heavily, and rumour had it that he was well nigh infallible. Almost all of us had accosted him at one time or another, hoping to pry out of him some little gem of inside information that would enable us to say goodbye forever to lifting heavy scripts and toiling over hot microphones, but invariably Bert would merely shift the rotten vegetable to the other side of his mouth and adopt a faint Mona Lisa smile. Bert was never one to run off at the mouth even at the best of times. It came as a bolt out of the blue, therefore, when he removed the cigar from his mouth one hot summer afternoon long enough to mouth audibly over the entire canteen, "Buy United States money."

It was as if Skookum Jim had just stumbled in from Bonanza Creek with his oversized nugget. Within two minutes the canteen was emptied and every office phone around the CBC had a wild-eyed embryo Rothschild barking his order for

U.S. money into the ears of bewildered bank tellers all over Toronto. Some CBC staff people, probably suffering from either obesity or heart conditions, were too late to get to a free office phone before the Toronto banks closed for the day. This precipitated a rash of long distance calls to either prairie banks or even West Coast banks that still remained open. All the transactions were completed through marginal buying; that is, the CBC people didn't put up any hard cash, but preferred to pay for their orders later on when they sold their skyrocketing U.S. dollars at enormous profit.

All that weekend around the studios a gleeful, collective hand-rubbing wore knuckles down to the bone. When Monday morning dawned and the banks opened again, the United States dollar had dropped to one of the lowest levels relative to the Canadian dollar in its history. And it languished, day after day, while Bert Pooler busied himself helping out in the canteen kitchen instead of taking his customary but more vulnerable place beside the cash register. After ten days the banks were beginning to clamour for the payments owing them, and the disillusioned CBC staffers had to cough up. By CBC standards everybody lost his shirt and the tearing of hair and rending of garments went on all the rest of that summer.

During my early years on CBC staff, my more impressionable years, I was inordinately sensitive to what seemed to be an attitude widely held among the general public toward males who worked for the CBC. It seemed to be a foregone conclusion that if you were employed by the CBC your vice was automatically versa. In those days, too, it didn't even help to plaster your hair with Brylcreem or drench your armpits with Right Guard, because television hadn't yet come along with its irrefutable system of standards for judging the virility and manliness of the North American male. Whenever at some social gathering I was approached by a stranger who enquired about my occupation, I had to resort to squaring my jaw, dropping my voice to its lowest possible register and, if I were sitting, crossing one leg over the other in order to expose a portion of hirsute calf above the sock line, before answering that I was employed by the CBC.

Considering such sensitivity, you can imagine how appalled I was one day to walk into the reception lobby of the radio building, where there were always half a dozen non-radio people sitting around waiting for various appointments, and discover the largest vending machine I have ever seen in my life, with a huge sign affixed to the front blatantly proclaiming FRUIT MACHINE. After peering in through its glass front I was considerably relieved to see mobile trays of apples, oranges, pears, and plums, but I couldn't help wondering how many of the general public would take the time to make a similar investigation before racing back to their respective places of business, babbling to their associates that the CBC was not only infested but, by God, automated. With all the available automatic vending machines to choose from — candy, coffee, sandwich, coke, etc. — I thought that one was particularly unfortunate and ill-advised. I had never seen one before, nor have I seen one since.

Fortunately, it lasted less than a week, and for its premature demise I'll be eternally grateful to Joe Niosi, the big, affable, and best known string bass player in Canada. During a rehearsal break one day, Joe lumbered out of Studio G along with about twenty of his fellow musicians and headed down the hall for the reception lobby where I happened to be sitting, broodingly contemplating the offending FRUIT MACHINE. Joe went over to the machine, set the selection indicator at the word APPLE, and then popped in his dime. As the individual trays of fruit began to slowly move in their elliptical orbit, a promising symphony of electronic whirrings and hummings began somewhere in the machine's entrails and offered high hope that something exciting was going to be disgorged any moment. After several seconds all sound and movement within the machine stopped, and Joe was left standing there with his huge palm open expectantly right under the orifice. A second dime was dropped in, and then a third, but still the beast gave no indication that it was planning to part with any of the fruit of its womb.

Without giving the slightest external indication that great buckets of adrenalin were gushing forth into his exasperated

MAX FERGUSON

arterial system, Joe placidly removed the soggy, mangled cigar from his mouth, grasped the sides of the machine between two massive, anthropoid arms, and shook it so violently that every single piece of fruit came cascading down the chute and out the opening. By the time they pulled Joe off the poor machine it was completely empty, and the floor of the lobby was swimming in apples, oranges, plums, and pears. Immediately a swarm of musicians, most of whom I'd seen dozens of times playing with the utmost grace and stateliness for the Toronto Symphony, had dropped to their hands and knees and were frantically cramming every available pocket. So disgusting was the undignified display of greed and gluttony that by the time I realized what was happening and had flung myself clawing and shoving into their midst, there was nothing left but a couple of badly crushed oranges.

When Joe Niosi wasn't wrecking fruit machines you could generally find him sitting over a cup of coffee in the CBC canteen, and I used to love to pull up a chair and listen to him recalling his boyhood days in our mutual home town of London, Ontario, where he grew up with the Lombardo boys. My favourite of a seemingly endless flow of anecdotes was the one about young Carmen Lombardo being thrown down a flight of stairs by his music teacher.

Both the Niosi and the Lombardo boys studied music in a walk-up studio on London's main thoroughfare, Dundas Street. Their teacher was an irascible Italian gentleman of the old school, imported through the collective efforts of London's Italian families to drum into the heads of their children, by whatever means he saw fit, an appreciation and working knowledge of music. The one thing the maestro couldn't abide was a student turning up without having properly prepared his lesson. It was for this very sin that he bounced a terrified young Carmen Lombardo down every step of the front stairway and right out onto Dundas Street. Within fifteen minutes Poppa Lombardo burst wild eyed into the studio, and while the tear-stained face of young Carmen peered out from behind his sheltering pant legs, the old man demanded to know why his boy had been thrown bodily down the front stairs.

94

When the truth was out, Carmen made his second painful trip of the day down the same stairway, this time flailed every inch of the way by his father's stout leather belt.

Since hearing that story I find I'm much more tolerant of that sobbing, whimpering vibrato which still persists in Carmen's adult singing voice, as its origins no doubt trace back to that one traumatic day in his young musical life. I kept listening to Joe's anecdotes, hoping out of Christian charity to discover a similar exoneration for Guy.

About two years ago I was watching on my TV screen, along with a good many other Canadians, a production of Hamlet filmed by the BBC. It was a brilliantly conceived production, further enhanced by the fact that the entire action was filmed in the massive old halls and fog-enshrouded ramparts of Elsinore Castle in Denmark. A second feature which undoubtedly assured its success was the choice of Christopher Plummer as Hamlet. I imagine it is now generally conceded that Plummer shares with Burton and Olivier the honour of being one of the world's three greatest Shakespearian actors.

For ninety minutes the combined magic of Shakespeare, Plummer, and the camera's eye had lifted me out of time and place and held me captive there at Elsinore in the very midst of those protagonists of Shakespeare's classic tale. In the few remaining moments of this total involvement we were all being propelled breathlessly toward that electrifying climax. Gertrude, having sipped the poisoned wine, lay dead before me. Laertes, a few feet away, lay sprawled where Hamlet's lethal thrust had despatched him. Hamlet, having just withdrawn his blade from the breast of the treacherous king, was himself sinking fast from the wound of Laertes' envenomed sword. Soon I was mentally echoing Horatio's anguished farewell to his sweet prince and beseeching flights of angels to sing him to his rest. The lifeless body of Hamlet was now being borne past me, his face pale and serene in death's repose, and then it happened. For no reason at all, except sheer perversity, my mind suddenly recalled an earlier calamity which had befallen this very same Prince of Players when, seated in the privacy of my living room, he had had an entire chocolate cake ground slowly and exquisitely into his face.

Plummer, on that particular occasion, had arrived at my apartment door for a social visit. He had brought with him a friend of his, another struggling young Toronto actor named Michael Kane. During the course of the evening while coffee was being served, my wife produced an immense chocolate cake which she asked Michael Kane to carry from the kitchen to the living-room table for cutting. It was a very small apartment and Kane had only about ten feet to walk before delivering his precious load safely to the table. But fate had decreed that his route take him past the chair on which Plummer was sitting, and as Kane passed by, Plummer asked, innocently enough, the flavour of the cake. To any normal person the simple answer, "Chocolate," would have sufficed, but to Michael Kane, whose body chemistry was very precariously balanced, it seemed quite logical that the most convincing way of answering such a question would be to take the cake and grind it slowly into the face of the enquirer. Which he did.

Michael Kane, who was without doubt the strangest person I've ever known, possessed every bit as much acting potential as Chris Plummer. The voice was just as resonant and expressive, and the face, except for a wild Béla Lugosi glint around the eyes, was much more ruggedly handsome. However producers around the CBC were a bit wary of using him because of his reputation for unpredictability and his predilection for slipping pages out of actors' scripts during the actual broadcast of a drama. When you begin a speech at the bottom of page 14 and finish it on the top of page 21 it doesn't always make sense.

I first heard of him in connection with an incident which took place in the CBC canteen many years ago. Kane had come into the canteen for coffee. The place was jammed and Kane made for the last remaining seat. In order to reserve it while he picked up his coffee at the self-serve counter, he removed his old air force bomber jacket and hung it over the back of the empty chair. While he was getting his coffee, the number three executive in the CBC hierarchy, Ernest Bushnell, Director

General of Programs, came into the canteen and made for what appeared to be an empty chair. He suddenly noticed the disreputable old bomber jacket with its dirty sheepskin collar and cracked leather sleeves sticking out grotesquely as if a pair of badly broken arms were still in them. Kane used to boast that the relic was so old and stiff with grime that it always assumed the exact shape of the last contortion he went into before slipping out of it.

Bushnell testily asked the assembled throng of canteen patrons who owned the jacket. Kane, at this moment, was just arriving back with his coffee and proceeded to answer Bushnell's ill-humoured query in a voice that was heard all over the canteen. "It's mine but I'm sorry, it's not for sale. Believe me, I'd like to let you have it, but there are so many memories wrapped up in that jacket that it can't be bought at any price. I'm terribly sorry. I know how disappointed you're going to be, but it just isn't for sale." Bushnell, unaccustomed to being answered back even civilly, almost gagged on this facetious and intentionally insolent misinterpretation of his original question. His face reddening, he dressed Kane down severely and told him that the canteen was for the use of CBC staff and that, as a freelance actor, he had no business being there.

Two days later, on a Saturday morning, Kane and Plummer pulled up in front of the Kremlin (the affectionate name by which the CBC executive headquarters on Jarvis Street is known) in an old truck which they'd rented. They had a couple of dozen sheep in the back, which they'd rented from a farmer, and they planned to herd them into Bushnell's office and leave them there for the weekend. Bushnell, upon opening his office door on Monday morning, would be greeted by a great derisive chorus of "baaahhhhs". The plan died a-borning when they found the Kremlin locked up tight for the weekend, and Kane was plunged into the depths of a brooding blue funk for days afterwards.

Much more successful than the thwarted retribution which they'd planned for Ernest Bushnell was a most imaginative venture they set out on together a short time later. This one was more than just an inane prank. It had overtones of social comment as eloquent as anything Dickens ever wrote.

The purpose of the experiment was to discover whether or not Torontonians had any concern or feeling for their fellow men. When Toronto citizens step over or walk around a heart attack victim lying in need of help on a Yonge Street sidewalk, when they gather in groups like slack-jawed humanoids to watch a policeman (or, for that matter, a woman) being beaten up by a gang of young punks, are they really being callously indifferent or, deep down inside, are they at war with themselves — torn between an instinctive desire to help and a long standing Anglo-Saxon tradition of reserve and aloofness which has made it a tribal taboo to show emotion in public?

Kane and Plummer felt that the answer might be found on a Yonge Street trolley which they boarded one afternoon, posing as a pair of country bumpkins who were visiting Toronto for the first time. In loud rural accents which none of the passengers could possibly miss, they made it clear that they wanted to get off at Grosvenor Street. (They pronounced it Gross-venner.) For the balance of the trip down Yonge Street they talked excitedly about the wonders of the big city, rushing across the aisle now and again to lean over some horrified gentleman's lap to get a better view of a particularly tall building. They gleefully counted every picture house they saw, and whenever a large delivery van would pass they'd try to calculate how many stocks of hay it would hold. Every now and then they would pause in their oo-ing and ah-ing long enough to remind each other to be on the lookout for Gross-venner Street because it was very important that they didn't miss it.

When they were about three blocks from Grosvenor Street a few restless fidgetings and throat clearings were heard from the passengers. A block away from Grosvenor Street, while the pair of them stood pressing their noses against the window to get a better look at the biggest aeroplane they'd ever seen, the uneasiness of the passengers became even more pronounced. Legs were crossed and uncrossed, anxious eyes peered out over the rim of newspapers, and the throat clearing

98

became deafening. When finally, as planned, the streetcar carried the unwitting pair of country visitors right past their Grosvenor Street stop, it was as if a strange collective urge to visit a bathroom had suddenly gripped the entire streetcar. It was the psychological moment for Kane and Plummer to twist the knife.

"See any sign sayin' Gross-venner yet?"

"Nope, but don't worry none cuz somebody's bound to tell us."

Kane and Plummer stayed on for several more blocks, enjoying every moment of the agonized symphony of communal guilt and then got off very slowly, casting long looks of hurt and reproach over their shoulders as they dawdled on the treadle step. But they had found their answer. Torontonians may not show it, but, by George, they care!

A few short weeks after the above sociological experiment the streetcars had stopped running and Yonge Street was being torn up in preparation for Toronto's new subway. No one quite knew just how far Yonge Street's face lifting was going to go, and a lot of shop-owners whose premises were situated on Toronto's main artery were a bit apprehensive. John Drainie told me of going into a tiny Greek restaurant on Yonge Street with Michael Kane one day. While they were paying their bill, Kane turned away from the proprietor and gave the premises a long, hard, calculating look. "Yeah, that seems to be the best way of doing it all right," he said, "the public washrooms can go right where those booths are, and we can run the spur line right through to the back, parallel with this counter." Kane then turned and walked toward the door, followed by an embarrassed John Drainie who looked back over his shoulder just once to see a robot-like hand dejectedly removing a half-chewed cigar from a slack lower jaw which hung open in a horrified face.

You'd think that would have been enough for one day, but they hadn't walked three blocks up Yonge Street when Kane veered abruptly off the sidewalk and walked out into the centre of Yonge Street to where a labourer was resting his pelvic bone on the handle of an air hammer and performing an exaggerated version of St. Vitus' Dance. Bellowing to make himself heard over the deafening staccato of the air hammer, Kane delivered into the labourer's left ear, "What provisions are being made for the concrete-reinforced vents every forty feet?" The poor startled worker, only out from Europe long enough to have managed an answer to "Is your aunt's pen on the table?", was totally unequipped to provide a proper answer to such an impressive, if unintelligible, query. Instead he smiled a confused little smile and called out in some middle-European accent to another man a few yards away. This man not only knew English, but was also several notches up in the social hierarchy of the labour force on which the Toronto Transit Commission was relying to get the subway built. Yet in spite of such credentials, he looked just as stunned as the immigrant labourer when Kane brazenly repeated his question regarding the phoney concrete-reinforced vents. He must have felt, though, that whatever they were, those concrete-reinforced vents were pretty important, because he promised to check them out with the foreman and went running off on the double. Kane then sauntered off up Yonge Street, and to this day the interlude has probably never again entered his mind.

I learned some time after this, on very good authority, that the ramifications of that piece of Michael Kane drollery made themselves felt in the top executive offices of the TTC. No doubt some distraught engineers had to spend quite a few hours over the original blueprints to convince the TTC that their subway would *not* cave in if they pushed on as planned and forgot all about those damned concrete-reinforced vents every forty feet.

I can readily appreciate that a steady diet of Michael Kane's erratic behaviour would be completely exhausting and overpowering. Fortunately I was able to enjoy his sporadic outbursts around the CBC radio building during the day and then, at the end of my stint, escape to the comparative quiet and sanity of my home and family. Not quite so blessed were the handful of haggard Toronto actors and writers who lived twenty-four hours a day cheek by jowl with him in the various coach houses, outhouses, and what-have-you that formed part of a converted estate just west of Toronto. Apparently he was worse out there than he was around the studios.

I can recall former Toronto writer, Ted Allan, wearily shaking his head over a cup of coffee in the CBC canteen and describing for me a small social soiree he had attempted to hold in his living room the previous evening for a few of his more stable and orthodox friends who were not connected with radio. The evening had started auspiciously. As his guests settled back comfortably, nursing their drinks, Ted cast a quick, apprehensive glance out through the open living room window across the expanse of communal lawn that adjoined all the homes in the little community. He was delighted to observe that the domicile that housed Michael Kane, his wife, and six children was in complete darkness. Kane had either gone to bed or was out. In either case, there would be no danger of one of his uninvited informal visits, which were always heralded by a human leg appearing out of the night and thrusting itself over the sill of the open window.

On one past occasion, after gaining entry in this fashion, Kane had walked silently around Ted Allan's living room, whisking partly consumed drinks out of the hands of startled guests. After amassing an armful of glasses, he disappeared through the window and across the lawn to his own party which, unfortunately, had run short of glasses. On another occasion the night visitor had burst in out of nowhere over the window sill of singer Charles Jordan's living room. This time the quest was for eggs. Kane walked silently and purposefully past Jordan's guests, helped himself to a bowlful of eggs in the kitchen, and then returned to the open living-room window, pausing long enough to break an egg over the head of Jordan's young son. While the goo slithered down over the boy's face like an obscene glacial cap, Kane disappeared into the night, leaving Jordan the task of offering some rational explanation of the charade to his stunned guests.

It was the vivid memory of such incidents that made Ted Allan so immensely relieved to look out and see the Kane home in darkness, realizing that he could enjoy with his friends an evening of gracious living and stimulating conversation without trepidation. Soon the nimble interplay of keen minds, honed to a fine edge by the subtle sharpening of good liquor, was filling the room with sparks of intellectual fire. Through the open window gentle breezes bore in from afar the soothing sounds of a summer night — the distant bark of a dog, the faint stirring of leaves, the tiny, soporific chant of a cricket chorus and then, from some source close by, a sort of banshee wail monotonously proclaiming, "Ted Allan is a poop! ... Ted Allan is a poop!"

The appalled host quickly glanced out of the window and spotted the dark silhouette of what appeared to be a large raccoon nestling in the uppermost branches of a tall tree outside the window. It was Michael Kane. Vaulting over the window sill, Allan raced out onto the lawn and hissed up at the shadowy figure to stop the nonsense immediately and come down. Kane ignored him and merely increased the volume of his disparaging chant. Realizing that he wasn't going to get Kane down out of the tree, Allan decided to compromise. He told Kane he could stay up in the tree if he would promise not to keep shouting that Ted Allan was a poop. Kane realized that Allan was not in a mood for joking, and after a few minutes of alternate threats and appeals he agreed not to persist in his defamation. Still smouldering, Allan returned to his guests, and in his role of a latter-day Madame de Sevigny, tried to salvage the badly shattered intellectual tone of the discussion. Meanwhile Kane, true to his promise, had begun to make amends by shouting, "Ted Allan is *not* a poop!" This revised hosanna from on high continued to drift in with unremitting regularity, drenching like a garden hose those precious sparks of intellectual fire, until the last of the literati had made his excuse for an early withdrawal and vowed listlessly that they must all get together again soon.

My last memory of Michael Kane before he moved away from Toronto was the look of utter disdain he shot me when I encountered him in a CBC studio and explained that I wouldn't be able to accept his invitation to accompany him to a giant Billy Graham faith rally at the CNE stadium to have my hernia faith-healed. Kane's plan, to which I originally agreed before losing my nerve, entailed offering ourselves from the audience to accept the laying on of hands. In actual fact, Kane had a bad back and I, indeed, had a hernia. We were going to let Billy Graham go through the motions of healing our afflictions. Then Kane had choreographed the whole affair so that we would walk jubilantly across the stage with bouncing, zestful steps before collapsing in a writhing heap of agony, Kane grabbing his back and I my groin. The thought of attempting to bring such a thing off in front of several hundred thousand believers forced me to back out at the last moment, and I'm sure Kane will never forgive me. I realize he may never return to Toronto, but I have a huge tree in front of my house and it worries me.

VI

A S THE RAWHIDE Little Theatre presentation gradually became more ambitious and complex, and as the listening audience began to increase with the extension of the program's coverage to the full network right across Canada, so the demands on my preparation time became more and more onerous. There were the half dozen or so esoteric ethnic recordings to hunt up each day (cowboy music had been dropped about 1950, thanks to the surprising and welcome results of an audience vote), there was the mail to be answered from all parts of Canada and the northern half of the United States falling within range of the CBC transmitters, and most time consuming of all, there was the Marvin Mellobell "production" to be conceived and written out. Once this was written, the necessary sound effects had to be picked out and my operator briefed on where these would have to come in during the skit. Something had to give and I'm afraid it was the efficiency of the announcing duties I performed for the CBC. Sometimes a station call or corporation cue would be missed while I was down in the record library ferreting out its hidden treasures. Often, after introducing a school broadcast, I would slip away to the sound-effects library to spend the ensuing half hour picking out the next day's sound effects. After what seemed to me to be no more than ten minutes I would be startled by the head of an irate producer sticking through the door and wanting to know where the hell I'd been twenty minutes ago when the school broadcast ground to its conclusion without the benefit of an announcer's sign-off.

The year 1953 was to become the winter of the CBC's discontent, and by the spring of 1954, the bubbling lava of official indignation finally erupted. For several months "fault reports" had been turning up with increasing regularity in my mail slot in the announcers' lounge. These were official printed forms which began with all the jocular levity of the Old Testament: YOU HAVE BEEN CHARGED WITH THE FOLLOWING ERROR. The offender would then have his guilt specifically set forth in longhand, and then it was back to the printed form for ERROR ACCEPTED ___, ERROR NOT ACCEPTED ___ . The two blanks were there to accommodate a check mark denoting innocence or guilt. Should you decide not to capitulate but go down with all guns firing, you then moved down to the bottom of the form where it said REASON FOR ERROR. The CBC had left sufficient space here so that anyone accustomed to copying out the Bible on the head of a pin would be able to get in a fairly good defence.

Ugly rumours were continually circulating among the older announcers that these fault reports were all entered on your PERSONAL FILE, which was locked away in some subterranean crypt at CBC headquarters in Ottawa. For this reason we would all try desperately to cram in at least a fragment of the most heartrending story we could devise in the hope that some flint-heart in Ottawa might be moved sufficiently to withhold the incriminating entry of his quill pen in the BIG BOOK and keep untarnished the reputation of all those Tiny Tims of the Toronto announce staff. Only one announcer, the all-time bête noir of the CBC, Allan McFee, scorned this craven behaviour. McFee owned one of those multicolour pens, which he used solely for writing the word "Poop" in five different, saucy colours over each of the many fault reports that found their way into his mail slot. A weary CBC secretary once told me it was a full-time job to retrieve these desecrations each day from the supervisor's desk before he saw them.

On that spring morning of 1954 when I was finally summoned to the office of a CBC executive, I knew full well what the subject of his remarks would be. Never in a million years, though, could I have anticipated the enormity of the indictment he hurled at me the second I came through the door. I was told that I had become the first announcer to supplant Allan McFee as the worst offender on the fault sheet. My first incredulous reaction was to blurt out that he must have his figures wrong, but they were all there, lying on his desk in black and white.

Almost any employee in any region of the CBC's far-flung empire will understand immediately my shocked disbelief at learning that I had exceeded Allan McFee in inefficiency of service rendered to the Corporation — such is his legendary ill-fame. To impart to a non-member of the CBC family, however, the extreme unlikelihood of anyone's ever achieving such a distinction, the bizarre chronicle of McFee's eccentric interpretation of his duties to the CBC would have to be set forth. This would entail several volumes and someday, if I'm still around when McFee has gone to that Great Studio in the Sky, I might write them. Certainly such a literary effort could never be decently undertaken in McFee's lifetime. There are too many McFee anecdotes which, if divulged openly, even at this late date, would likely result in his immediate

Max (r) and Allan McFee

dismissal from the CBC.

His favourite line of self-pity used to be, "When I consider how my days are spent, squatting like a toad in this foetid little cell, waiting for that challenging moment every half hour to say 'CBL, Toronto,' I'm engulfed in black clouds of depression." I know for a fact, though, that McFee during his hours of duty in CBL studio did much more than merely squat like a toad. Quite early in his CBC career he discovered that, by simply opening his microphone in that "fetid little cell", he could send his voice out over whatever program the CBC was airing at the time.

It would not be an exaggeration to say that McFee's voice has turned up at one time or another, completely unauthorized, on just about every program on the CBC schedule. The incongruously masculine and terribly vulgar throat clearing that Ma Perkins gave after a sweet word to Willie and Shuffle, the stentorian nose blowing which would accompany a celestial French horn passage in a symphonic performance ... all came from the toad in his fetid cell. His speciality was a sound so obnoxious and startling that I've literally jumped at hearing it issuing forth from my radio in the privacy of my living room. He usually reserved it for the caesural pause in poetry readings or as a follow-up to such inviting dramatic dialogue as, "John, darling, this will come as a shock, but I've felt for a long time now that you must hear it!" Strangely enough, McFee was able to lay all these rude little eggs like a malicious cuckoo-bird in the nests of unsuspecting producers and they were never traced to him. They were always faithfully and erroneously entered into the CBC daily log as "unidentified noise on the line". That is, with the exception of one nightmarish occasion when his diversionary pastime backfired.

The story was told to me by J. Frank Willis who, like a latter-day venerable Bede, seems to have mentally chronicled everything that ever happened in the CBC. The incident occurred some years before I arrived on the Toronto scene back in the days when the CBC, as part of its late afternoon radio fare for kiddies, used to receive by direct line from New York and transmit over its Toronto station a dramatized version of the comic strip, *Terry and the Pirates*. The program always opened with a noisy Chinese street scene — a cacophonous melange of rickshaw wheels, gongs, and shrill Chinese voices which lasted for about fifteen seconds before the U.S. announcer came in. During this period, McFee would open his mike and in a sing-song Chinese voice send out all his repressions toward the CBC and its executives in some rather salacious and defamatory language. The listeners at home, of course, were never able to distinguish McFee's libellous catharsis from the general noise of the Chinese street scene which camouflaged it. However, the routine had a rather effective shock value from the studio end. Anyone who happened to tiptoe into the studio while it was in progress would hear only McFee and not the U.S. origination, since the studio speakers always cut off when a microphone is opened. There would be McFee sitting in front of an open microphone sending out over 50,000 watts of power some pretty awful things about the CBC and the men who ran it. Frank Willis, having seen the stunt pulled on several occasions by McFee, knew that it was quite harmless, but the fun lay in watching the face of anyone not in the know who might slip into the studio while McFee was in the middle of it. One day as McFee was in the middle of his act, chanting, "O yang quong kee… stupid old CBC … soo yung … crazy knuckle-head (censored name of CBC executive) … him velly dumb, velly useless … sit on big fat bum all day … do nothing … o yang soo …" and so on, Willis noticed that the operator in the control room seemed to be in a bit of a frenzy as he gesticulated through the glass trying to get McFee's attention. Willis hastily alerted McFee with a dig in the ribs; McFee then cut his microphone to restore the speaker feed of *Terry and the Pirates,* and they both listened. There was stony silence. Where normally there would have been a noisy Chinese crowd scene, there was absolutely nothing, due to a failure in the transmission of the program from New York. McFee's virtuoso performance had been going out over 50,000 watts with not a sound to disguise it.

For anyone else such a traumatic experience would have

served as an object lesson, but when I came to Toronto some years later, the only noticeable disciplinary effect the incident had produced on McFee was that he had abandoned recognizable spoken words and was now relying solely on throat clearings, nose blowings, and that previously mentioned loathsome sound to herald his uninvited appearance on just about every program that went out over the CBC Toronto transmitters.

It is only fair to mention that, on the credit side, there has been during the last three or four years a noticeable change for the better in Allan McFee. He's still far from what you'd call a "company man", but a great deal of the former perverseness and destructive drive has gone. I won't attempt to offer any psychological reasons, but I'm convinced the personality change has something to do with getting rid of his dreadful old car, which for years must have been the most uncared for, mistreated, and shockingly dilapidated wreck on the streets or Toronto. One of my earliest recollections of McFee was seeing him in the back parking lot behind the Jarvis Street studios one morning, slowly walking around his car and methodically kicking dents in all four fenders. When I asked him what the trouble was, that suave, well-modulated, rich, warm, sincere voice that I'd heard so often on network radio explained very rationally, without a trace of malice, that the car had been reluctant to start that morning. As punishment he had driven it down at top speed without changing out of low gear and now was administering the final discipline so that such a thing wouldn't happen again. The frightening part of it was that he made it all sound so plausible and reasonable ... a perfectly natural thing to do to a mass of disobedient steel.

After exposing me to my first encounter with this "battered car syndrome", McFee backed the poor beast tight against the wall of the CBC building and left it with the engine running while he walked off. I called after him to draw his attention to what I foolishly assumed was an oversight, but once again the explanation was a very simple and straightforward one. He always left the car engine running. He was hoping to asphyxiate a certain CBC producer who, months previously, had reported him to CBC management for some infraction of CBC regulations. Every single day since that time, he had patiently parked his car in the same spot — tight against the studio wall, with the exhaust pipe pressed flush against a tiny air intake which led to Studio H. The engine was then left running for the entire day in the hope that the offending producer might just by some chance be assigned to a show in the polluted studio when the right amount of carbon monoxide had accrued. Fortunately, since Studio H was a fairly large studio, the right amount never did accrue, and the CBC was spared McFee's gaseous rendition of the Guy Fawkes Plot. However, during one of the Royal Tours which occurred at this time an entire program crew, working on the preparation of a nightly show called Royal Tour Diary, had to be evacuated from studio H when the producer smelled heavy concentrations of car exhaust. The producer, over a cup of coffee in the CBC canteen the following morning, excitedly recounted to me the "close call" they'd had. To this day, or at least until the publishing of this book, he's had no idea where the car exhaust came from.

After about six months of sweetly anticipated revenge, Captain Ahab began to realize that it was costing him a full tank of gas a day to pursue his White Whale, so he finally abandoned the attempt. In view of the bitter disappointment this caused him, I was surprised one day to encounter him walking jauntily down the lower studio corridor, his face wreathed from ear to ear in a huge smile. He was in bubbling good humour and told me he'd just had one of the most satisfying and rewarding moments of his whole life. His face was literally radiant, and when he began talking about the "divine hand of God", I was almost convinced there'd been a religious conversion. It turned out, however, to be slightly more prosaic.

As the story unfolded, babbled with almost childlike delight, it turned out that he'd been waiting in his car for the light to turn green at the corner of Jarvis and Wellesley. Just as the light changed and he began to move out into the intersection, a car next to him in the curb lane began to cut him off in order to make an illegal left-hand turn from the wrong lane. McFee had often mentioned how he kept both front fenders permanently dented for the purpose of ramming such traffic offenders, and I could easily see what a golden moment this would be for him. Apparently, though, as he prepared to ram he noticed that a second car, immediately behind the first, was preparing also to make the same illegal left turn right across McFee's path. "I couldn't believe my luck," he beamed. "It was one of those rare moments, divinely arranged." It took infinite self-control and exquisite timing to hold off, but he waited until both cars were exposing their vulnerable fenders to his beady Richthofen eye, and then he accelerated. This, then, was what had occasioned what I had mistaken for religious ecstasy — the fact that, like the Brave Little Tailor, McFee had been able to get two with one blow.

The demise of the car and what I maintain was a resultant personality change came about four years ago, when McFee was approached by executives of the large automobile manufacturing company whose wares he'd been helping to sell on radio and TV for years. They patiently pointed out that the impetus which his compelling commercial voice was giving to their sales was being counteracted by his insistence on driving in public one of their models which they'd just as soon the buying public didn't see. It was what the advertising world calls "a negative image". And how right they were.

In addition to the rust-corroded dents, gouges, and scratches that covered the car like German measles, it travelled around Toronto streets dragging about six feet of what originally had been weather-stripping but what now looked like decaying mummy cloth. The floor boards had long since rotted away, and through the gaping holes you could see the road flashing by a foot below your feet. Although McFee would insist that the missing floorboards were actually a safety device, claiming that when he saw a series of sewer lids flying past underneath him he knew he was too close to the curb, for the average passenger it was a terrifying experience and one most conducive to vertigo. For a long time I couldn't understand why I got a strange feeling of nostalgia for the East Coast every time we rounded a corner in McFee's car. Then it dawned on me that there were several gallons of accumulated rainwater trapped somewhere under the back seat, and their slushing back and forth produced a pleasurable sound something akin to the opening of *Harmony Harbour.*

The old wreck has been gone for four years now, and in its place is a reasonably modern car which McFee never kicks or uses to ram other cars. During this same four-year period, with the exception of one inconsequential occasion when he turned on a fire hose inside the CBC, McFee's behaviour has been meticulous. Certainly in the four years he's been connected with my morning radio program I couldn't have asked for a better-behaved or more co-operative announcer. In this day and age it would be preposterous to suggest that a machine could exert an evil influence over a human being. Yet, within two weeks after he unloaded that wretched old car, I personally watched Alan McFee climb up on a chair in CBL studio and nail over top of a nude Varga Girl a wooden plaque whose words began, "Christ is the head of this house ... the silent listener to every conversation ...."

VII

MOTHER NATURE AND CBC management may strike some as rather strange bedfellows, but every spring around the old studios on Jarvis Street they joined forces to make this the most wonderful time of the year. While tiny young dandelions, plantain, and crabgrass poked tender green heads up through the cracks of Jarvis Street sidewalks, while the cooing and fluttering of newborn pigeons wafted down from the CBC eaves (along with pounds of guano), CBC management added its contribution to the gladsome feeling of regenerative new hope by issuing Annual Increments. These modest but most welcome salary increases, ranging from $100 to $140 annually, were awarded each Spring to staff members in good standing. Though some petulant churls referred to them as Annual Excrements, for most of us they were Mardi Gras and New Year's Eve rolled into one. In addition to the financial appeal, I also enjoyed the social aspect of Annual Increment Day. It was the one occasion each year when I was able to see and fraternize with all my fellow staff announcers. Normally, due to housemaid's knee, hangnails, and other incapacitating infirmities to which announcers fall prey, and also due to our working in shifts, we would rarely see more than three or four of our fellows on any given day. On Annual Increment Day, however, a gallant parade of the halt, the lame, and the blind would be seen filing into the supervisor's office with warm little palms held out expectantly. Some had even come in on their day off.

It was in the midst of such a gathering that I stood one late spring morning in 1954. As the most junior and lowest paid announcer on Toronto staff the visions of sugar plums were dancing in my head a bit more wildly than in others. One by one, my blood brothers marched out, giggling and triumphantly waving their little white slips of magic paper. Finally I was left standing alone before the supervisor, trembling with anticipation like Oliver Twist asking for that second bowl of gruel. I also had about as much success with my Mr. Bumble as Oliver had with his. It was explained to me that there was no Annual Increment because I had reached the top of my group.

Apparently CBC tribal custom decreed that any staff member who had advanced, step by step each year to the top of a group must then mark time until management considered his contribution sufficiently above the call of duty to warrant boosting him over into the bottom of the next group. My fellow announcers had long since moved on well into groups 7 and 8, and I was now left marooned at the top of group 6. When I had joined the CBC in 1946 one of the first things I did was to greedily project my expected earnings, allowing for an automatic increment each year, in a steady, step-by-step, upward climb. Totally unaware of such enforced periods of financial fallow as now confronted me, I had computed that at age 65 I would be making $6,000 per year. Now that I'd turned up this SORRY card and would be forced to miss a few turns, I could well reach the age of 98 before I completed the course and crossed the finish line to the big prize money. My only crestfallen comment to the supervisor was to ask how long I would be left dangling from that dizzy pinnacle of wealth that was the top of Group 6. His reply, which has always stayed with me verbatim, was, "Until something special happens." I tried to glean some tiny ray of hope from this cryptic, succinct rejoinder, but all that I could think of was the blooming of century plants and the Second Coming.

Later that day, after finishing my shift of announce duties, I went home to lick my wounds. After sitting at home for a few hours, nursing my wrath to keep it warm, I decided that since I'd donated the Rawhide program to the CBC for the past eight years without missing a broadcast, it wouldn't be overly vindictive of me if I were to stay home on this one occasion and miss that evening's Rawhide show. After all, I reasoned, I had already put in a full day at the announcer's job for which they were paying me. It would just mean their doing without their little bonus for one occasion.

At the time it seemed an innocuous enough reprisal. I can even recall seeing in it a strong resemblance to the little cockney in that old English joke ... the poor little fellow who had just discovered, for the tenth time, his wife in bed with his best friend, Alfie. This was a bit thick even for his easy-going temperament so, in a sudden and long-overdue release of pent-up rage and resentment, he raced out of the bedroom, stormed down the stairs into the kitchen, and there made two cups of tea, "One for myself, one for me wife, and to hell with Alfie!"

Some time before this, the Rawhide program had been moved from the mornings to an evening spot — 6:40 to 7:00 p.m. — and now as the broadcast hour approached, I settled back in front of my radio at home to see what kind of apology announcement would be made to explain the absence of old Rawhide. Earl Cameron was the duty announcer that evening, and it fell to his lot to do the explaining. "We reckon as how old Rawhide has moseyed off down the old corral this evening," said Earl, with about the same light-hearted frivolity as he would have used on the opening line of the National News. "But he's left a few of his favourite records lying around the old bunk-house, and we aim to play them for you."

The program was barely off the air when my phone rang and a rather blunt and testy managerial voice asked why in hell I wasn't down doing the Rawhide show. I thought the aggressive approach was a bit unjustified — perfectly understandable later, of course, when I divulged my reason for not showing up — but not as an opening gambit when, for all he knew, I might have been run over by a water-flusher, attacked by a rabid squirrel, or otherwise legitimately *hors de combat*. When he continued to press me for a reason, I was still in an easy-going mood and reluctant to confess that I had simply been mad at the CBC. Instead, I explained that on my CBC announcer's salary I could never quite make it from one payday to the next, and since my car was out of gas and I'd lost my credit card, there had been no way of getting down for the program on time. "Damn it," was the reply, "You've got a program to do, and you bloody well owe it to the CBC to do it!"

At this point I'm afraid I impetuously lumped my announcer's job, the Rawhide show, and himself into one big package deal and by personifying the CBC suggested a rather vulgar repository for the lot.

I've never been able to ascertain which crossed top management's desk first, his recommendation for my dismissal or my resignation. The next day I was summoned by another CBC executive who, smiling and affable, assured me that if I were only to apologize to the other official he was sure the order for my dismissal would be rescinded. However, having buttered my bread I decided to lie in it and told him I would never apologize.

Later in the day I was summoned by another executive, Harry J. Boyle, who was then head of the CBC's Trans Canada Network. I walked into the office of this rough-and-tumble, florid-faced bear whose bucolic exterior housed the scholarly and creative mind that had devised for the CBC most of its best radio fare, including the CBC *Wednesday Night* series. Harry had his feet up on his desk and was busily removing his lunch from a wrinkled old brown bag. "Well, what are you going to do now?" he drawled.

You could always level with Boyle so I quickly replied, "Just get out of the CBC, that all!"

His next question startled me, coming out of the blue from behind two slices of bread, whose contents he was sniffing disdainfully. "Why don't you sell your Rawhide program to the CBC?"

I laughed and assured him that, at this stage of events, if I came up with a cure for cancer the CBC wouldn't buy it from me.

"Well, why don't you go home and relax for a couple of days. I'll look into it for you."

Though he was head of the network, Harry Boyle had always seemed to identify more with program people than with management. He was well known and well liked for his willingness to tackle top management with any hopeless cause which lower-deck types were forever dropping into his lap. Within two days he called me to his office again to confirm that the CBC had agreed to buy the Rawhide program on a contract basis at approximately four times my announcer's salary. This meant, in addition, that as a free agent I could now live wherever I wanted in Canada as long as I delivered Rawhide five times a week to the network. I shook the hand of that grand old midwife, Harry J. Boyle, who had so efficiently severed the umbilical cord on whose other end lay the placenta of my CBC staff career. With all of Canada to choose from, including my own hometown of London, I headed immediately for the East Coast and arrived in Halifax with my family in a matter of days.

I've been asked dozens of times to explain this geographical predilection I have for the Maritimes. In almost every interview I can recall, there has been the same floundering attempt to rationally dissect and label the component parts of a strong emotion I feel for the Maritimes but find impossible to describe. I realize, of course, it has a lot to do with the sea. Allan McFee never misses a chance to taunt me with what he derisively calls my "subconscious return to the womb". At this very moment, writing sleepily in the small hours of the morning, the only sound I can hear is the muffled crashing of surf hurling itself against the craggy northern coast of Cape Breton just below my cottage window. To my ears, and I would imagine to most people's, it's one of the most therapeutic and hypnotic sounds in the world. What a wonderful joke on McFee if his flip, derisive little Freudianism should happen to have a ring of truth to it — if, indeed, the awesome sight and sound of the sea, life's earliest womb, stirred in our subconscious a dim recollection of that billion-year-old memory when Nature added a few more cells, coaxed us to slither up onto the land, and left us there with our life-giving sea now inside us instead of around us, now red instead of blue. Put that in your pipe and smoke it, McFee!

Combined with the sea, just as potent and awesome a spellbinder, is the history of the East Coast — not just history chronicled on the printed page, but history so palpable that it can be viewed with the eye and touched with the hand. The rows of little white crosses in Fairview Cemetery a few hundred yards from my Halifax home, each bearing the same stark date and nothing more, will always convey to me more poignantly than volumes of written history the agony of the *Titanic*'s last hour. The proud and formidable French fleet sent out before the fall of Louisburg to do great things for the French cause in the New World seemed unreal and hopelessly remote when I yawned over it in my high school text. Yet on that chilly fall night when I swam in the black, frigid water of Bedford Basin, the upper adjunct to Halifax Harbour, and realized suddenly that the ghostly and colossal ruin was still sleeping on in the mud a few fathoms below me, history was certainly close enough to add an additional shudder to that occasioned by the icy water.

I'll always remember the simple eloquence with which Fred Brickenden put into words so much of what I've felt and couldn't express about the lure of the East Coast. Brickenden was the CBC Halifax news editor whose deafening bellow, "Benefit of Sanctuary!" used to arrest Briggs in full flight whenever he was pursuing some fleeing miscreant who had sought out the haven of the newsroom. Like myself, he was a non-Maritimer who had started out with the CBC in Halifax and then been transferred to Toronto. In 1954, shortly before my own return as a freelancer, Brickenden was sent back as director of the Halifax television operation, which was just beginning. He described his return after several years of exile in Toronto. "After landing in Dartmouth I came across Halifax harbour by ferry sitting in the back of a TCA limousine. We turned up Hollis Street heading for the Nova Scotian Hotel. A steady Halifax rain, the wettest in all the world, was beginning to pelt down. Shrouds of opaque Halifax fog were rolling up over the city from the harbour. The smell of fish hung heavy in the air. To put the final brush stroke to the canvas, I glanced out of the limousine window and beheld a drunken sailor ricocheting along the length of a wooden fence and regurgitating as he went. It was too much. The flood gates opened and I threw up my hands in the back seat of the limousine. Joyously and for all the world to hear I cried, "I'm home! I'm home!"

And so, in that summer of 1954, I was home myself. Whatever it is about the East Coast — the sea, the history, the fog, the rain, the drunken matelots — it was like a tonic and immediately produced an exhilarating effect on both myself and, logically, the Rawhide program. The skits came readily and with little effort. Even today, when listeners write and recall some favourite escapade of the Rawhide characters, it invariably turns out to be from this second Halifax period from 1954 to 1958.

Granny was particularly hopped up during those years. She focussed all her resentment of Upper Canada on one poor innocent young girl, Marilyn Bell, who was merely doing her best to put Toronto on the map with her feats of marathon swimming. Granny, who made no bones about her seething jealousy of this young "upstart", flung herself into impossible tasks of Herculean labour to try to supplant Miss Bell in the headlines of the day. She became the first octogenarian to swim the Bay of Fundy backwards using only ears. She became the first person of any age to tunnel through the base of Citadel Hill, that great fortress guarding the entrance to Halifax Harbour from which it is said that no shot has ever been fired in anger, except on rainy days when the old fellow goes out to fire the noonday gun with a packet of soggy matches. It was during these Halifax-based years that Granny circumnavigated North and South America in a barrel. After each fresh triumph, when Marvin Mellobell would thrust his CBC microphone at her for a few modest words from a gracious champion, Granny would first of all hurl nasty taunts at Marilyn Bell, then go on to roast well-wishers across Canada for their failure to include deep-freezes, TV sets, and sports cars along with their congratulatory telegrams.

How I managed all this boisterous ebullience during those four years I'll never know, because my regular operator was an ex-undertaker named Carl Scott. He had the most mournful expression I've ever seen on a human being, and with his long face and sad, sad eyes, he always reminded me of a big lugubrious bloodhound who'd just been scolded for losing a scent. Carl would always track me down in some remote corner of the CBC Halifax building about five minutes to air time as I tried to utilize those all-important remaining minutes to map out the action and dialogue of the evening's skit. A lot of CBC Toronto types were prone to do the same thing, but with them it would always be the latest off-colour joke, snappily told and slickly larded with the latest hip expressions. Carl, unfortunately, drew his bon mots and little anecdotes rather ponderously from the one milieu he knew best — the world of the dead. Though they'd have been pure delight for any red-blooded young necrophiliac, they were hardly the sort of catalyst you'd seek out if you were due on the air in five minutes with a program of bubbling good fun. Since most of them were far too ghastly to repeat, you'll have to be content with the only one I can recall which comes anywhere close to making the category of good clean family fun.

On this particular occasion, Carl and his uncle had "put the boots to the big car" and arrived at an accident scene slightly in advance of the "big car" of a rival parlour in the same rural area of Nova Scotia. I gathered, from Carl, that the two rival enterprises operated on a sort of squatters' rights basis. Once back at the funeral parlour, the uncle discovered that among other injuries the victim was missing a left ear. Fortunately, as Carl put it, "The uncle was right handy with the mortician's wax." Working into the small hours of the next morning he fashioned quite a convincing replica of a left ear, "A helluva left ear," as Carl put it with justifiable pride. The deceased was then laid out in the viewing room, and the uncle had barely time to make his exit when in came the next-of-kin. A small boy ran ahead of the rest, and after spotting the deceased, jumped up and down, excitedly shouting to his mother that Uncle Arnold had a left ear. It turned out that the man never did have a left ear, having lost it accidentally somewhere around the age of four.

Top: Max, Rube Hornstein, and the Queen of the Seas Pageant Winner.
Bottom: Rube Hornstein, Tannis Anne Sedaro, and Max.

Promoting *Gazette.*
Fisheries Exhibition, Lunenburg, N.S., 1954

VIII

B Y LATE 1954, Canadian television, which had appeared innocently enough the previous year as only a tiny lump in Toronto's breast, had now begun to proliferate into most of the CBC regions across Canada and was well on its way to becoming that huge growth we recognize today — occasionally benign, generally malignant, but firmly imbedded in the soft receptive flesh of our society.

In addition to my Rawhide series on radio I found myself, in December of 1954, host of the first live program to be televised from the CBC Halifax studios to the Maritimes. It was a weather and interview program called *Gazette,* and it was to provide me with four of the most enjoyable and satisfying years of my career. Since Halifax is somewhat off the beaten path of show biz, there were very few vapid Hollywood cuties to contend with such as were to later turn up, with sickening and depressing regularity, when I was living in Toronto and interviewing nightly on the program, *701.* Instead, we chose our guests for *Gazette* from the raw material around us — unaffected, believable, and honest human beings who had a story to tell each night and told it with compelling interest and often, I must admit, embarrassing frankness and candour.

Typical of this run of guests was Bill Thompson, an elderly retired gentleman who was serving as a school crossing guard when I first heard of him. I had read with fascination in my high school years of the great Halifax explosion of 1917 and of the gallant little fire engine which had set off to put out the fire in the *Mont Blanc,* unaware of its deadly cargo of munitions, and I was amazed to discover that Bill Thompson had been the driver and sole survivor. He arrived at our TV studios carrying the twisted remnants of the steering wheel and launched into a gripping recollection of that terrible day in Halifax history. He told how the call had come in that a ship was on fire in Halifax harbour near Jetty 3, how they had started out from the fire hall, six of them on that December morning, in their brand new pumper, the *Patricia,* Halifax's first mechanized fire engine. None of them dreamed that this was to be anything other than a routine call.

Waiting for them at the end of their run, of course, was the *Mont Blanc,* a Belgian munitions ship which had collided with a Norwegian freighter at the Narrows, where Halifax harbour merges into Bedford Basin. With flames now rapidly engulfing her deadly cargo, she had drifted down-harbour and was alongside Jetty 3 as the proud little pumper approached. The indescribable explosion that killed all the pumper crew except Bill Thompson also brought thousand of startled Haligonians to their windows all over the city. It was here in this most vulnerable spot they were standing, peering out through the glass when, seconds after the explosion, the concussion wave reached them and was able to complete its work of death and destruction that much more efficiently. Then the entire harbour opened up, and a huge tidal wave rolled up over the waterfront and hurled itself at the stricken city. Along with the debris of fragmented ships and homes and stores, it carried Bill Thompson up from the waterfront and dumped him, bleeding and unconscious, in the middle of a street a couple of blocks away.

Throughout his retelling of this story I had been careful not to interrupt with any questions. None were needed. But now as he finished and I looked around at our hard-bitten staging and technical crew standing like enthralled statues, I said simply, "Mr. Thompson, that must have been a nightmarish experience." He looked at me blankly for several seconds while his mind returned to the present from that terrible day in 1917 and then very quietly he said, "You're god-damned right it was!" There wasn't a murmur of complaint from the viewing audience.

On another occasion I was to interview a tough, seasoned old merchant marine captain. We finished the rehearsal and, as usual, I went home for dinner before coming down to do the actual program at 7:00 p.m. During the course of our meal my wife asked who my guest was to be that evening. I told her it was a man named Captain Norman Smith. "Oh, for Heaven's sake! I went to school with his daughter! I'm sure that's Capt. Cussin' Norm." With a sinking feeling in my stomach, I enquired how he had come to get a nickname such as "Cussin' Norm" and learned that it was really quite simple and logical. He swore like a trooper. Within an hour, however, as I approached the end of my on-air interview with Captain Smith, I realized that my fears had been groundless. The man was obviously well aware that his voice and image were going out into the homes of thousands of decent Maritime families. There had, of course, been one or two tiny pauses here and there where he seemed to be mentally expurgating the spicy effects of a speech habit he'd cultivated during many years at sea. But the overall impression had been impeccable, and we were now almost home-free as he launched into his final anecdote concerning a wartime sailing from Boston to Halifax.

About half a day out of Boston, he explained, he observed off his starboard bow the conning tower and sleek grey hull of a U-boat breaking the surface. Through his loud-hailer, the U-boat commander ordered him to give his cargo and destination. At this stage in the anecdote I spotted the floor director giving me the ten second cue to wind up, and feeling safe and secure I tossed in the final question, "Did you give him the information, Captain Smith?" "Well," he replied, "my number one up there on the bridge turned to me and said, 'You're not gonna tell him are you, Cap'n Norm,' but I took another long look down the barrels of them guns they had trained on us and I says to my number one, 'You're goddamned right I'm gonna tell him!'" In spite of the stomach constrictions they gave me, I was later to pine for such guests as Bill Thompson and Captain "Cussin' Norm" Smith as I sat night after night in the Toronto studios of *701*, listening in utter boredom to the frothy, superficial, and totally unimportant details of some Hollywood "star's" stupid biography, gushingly delivered in very proper and very affected stage English.

Four years of nightly interviewing on *Gazette* involved me in more preposterous and uproarious situations than I've encountered in all the other years of my life combined. Some, of course, had to be enjoyed in retrospect and certainly didn't seem funny at the time. There was the evening, for example, during the early weeks of the program, when I began an interview with a guest who had also brought along his horse and his dog. We made quite a nice little grouping, the man and myself standing together, the huge stallion standing beside us, and the big, fat, out-of-condition boxer lying on the floor in front of the horse. We had only one studio camera in those days, and as the interview began, our producer chose a medium-length shot of the guest and myself. Two minutes into the interview, when the guest referred to his dog, the producer called for the single camera to pan down off the guest and myself, along the floor and offer the viewers a shot of the animal in question. However, when the camera arrived on the beast, he was busily engaged in performing some very personal and aesthetically offensive ablutions which one could scarcely offer up to a dinnertime viewing audience.

On the orders of the producer, the camera retraced its steps and came panning back along the floor to rest again on my guest and myself. It wasn't to stay there very long, however, since my guest, more used to the company of animals than humans, had chosen that very moment to commence a most diligent search for something he'd lost and which, for some unknown reason, he seemed to think might be found somewhere in the vicinity of his left nostril. Realizing that his efforts at creative cinematography had degenerated into a game of musical chairs which he was fast losing, the frantic producer decided to despatch the camera toward the last remaining chair — the huge stallion patiently standing beside us. Earlier in the afternoon it had taken three hours to lead this skittish leviathan, blindfolded, into the studio. The entire television building had to be evacuated of all bodies so that his highly strung temperament wouldn't be upset by any extraneous voices. Yet as the camera started to pan along his great body, it became horribly obvious to all of

125

us that he was finding the world of television not too upsetting an environment after all. In fact, so relaxed and nonchalant had he become that he was now sleepily lost in the equine delights of an erotic reverie, the physical manifestation of which seemed to give the impression that he was standing on five legs. Our last photographic escape route had been cut off, and bowing to the dictates of common decency, the camera came to a grinding halt somewhere along the rib cage, about a foot short of the offending member. There it stayed, not daring to move, for the remainder of the voice-over interview. That one was always referred to later as The Night of the Horrid Threesome.

One of the most painful interviews I can remember doing on *Gazette* was with a lady called Mrs. Thomas. She had phoned one day and asked if she might come on the program to talk about ocelots, a variety of small leopard used in Venezuela for hunting. She arrived on the set that evening with a live ocelot on a leash. Having observed it for about ten minutes hissing, spitting, growling, and lunging at anyone who came within five feet of it, I was a bit uneasy when I learned that Mrs. Thomas planned to have it with her all through our interview. She assured me that it would lie quietly at our feet and to put my fears at rest, she had brought along a big bone, which she planned to give to the ocelot when the interview started.

Sure enough, the interview went quite smoothly, with the ocelot curled up contentedly, munching on its bone just beside my right foot. Mrs. Thomas was a charming personality. She was personable and knew her subject well. Certainly, what I could hear of her through the growls, bone splintering, and chop smacking coming up from the floor seemed most interesting. I think my mistake was in letting the interview run on longer than planned, because somewhere along the line the ocelot had finished tearing off all the edible portions of meat from the bone and was looking around for seconds. It was while he was in this restless mood that I happened to move my right foot, indicating to the ocelot, no doubt, that the object he'd seen out of the corner of his eye was indeed alive.

With an angry snarl he hurled himself at my ankle and, taking the whole thing in his jaws, crunched down hard. My first

Gazette
(top to bottom) Rube Hornstein,
Max, Don Tremaine

reaction to the excruciating pain was to reach down and pry off his jaws with my hands. Just as I made my lunge, Mrs. Thomas offered her memorable advice, "Oh, don't do that! You might make him angry." Like a fool I followed her advice and let him have his way with my ankle to preserve his "good natured" mood. Trying to ignore the pain, I pressed on with the interview, until the growls and slavering became so loud you could hardly hear our voices. By now the camera had "dollied in" for a close-up and our dinner-time viewers were treated to a charming shot, full screen, of the scarlet stain now oozing through and spreading over my light-coloured socks.

Mrs. Thomas, all the while, was offering advice, stressing that the most important thing was not to anger the ocelot, and that if we could just manage to ignore the little fellow, he'd soon tire of his attention-getting behaviour. Since the ocelot gave no indication that he would tire much before he'd worked his way up to my thigh, I decided to run the risk of being called a rotten sport and eventually grabbed his jaws in my hands, pried him off, and handed him, spitting, hissing, and clawing, to his mistress.

As far as I can recall there was only one other evening of bloodletting on *Gazette*. It occurred during the height of the Hungarian Revolution, when hundreds of Hungarian refugees were being landed in Halifax. We had learned that among these people there happened to be a young man who was the Intercollegiate Fencing Champion of Hungary. We felt it would be interesting to bring him on *Gazette* and devote the evening to an interview on the subject of fencing. It took us only five minutes, after he arrived at the studios, to realize that we had a real prima donna on our hands. He was a haughty, demanding, and imperious young man whose sullen, scowling face spat out even the words "Good evening" as if they were an order. On the other hand, all of us connected with the program were simply dripping with charm and good-fellowship, grinning from ear to ear, offering him coffee and cigarettes so that he couldn't possibly mistake our little TV program for an MKVD interrogation.

The producer explained to him that I would question him about fencing, and that throughout the body of the interview he would have a chance to explain the various aspects of the sport. "After the interview portion is finished," the producer went on, "we would like to have you and Max stand up so that you can demonstrate on Max all the techniques you've been talking about. You'll each have an epee, and it should provide a nice, light ending to the program." But young Bela Lugosi was having none of this and chewed out the producer for offering up to him such an unworthy adversary on whom to demonstrate his skill. Finally the producer resorted to that old traditional North American argumentative technique, money. At the first mention of the ten-dollar honorarium connected with the interview, several centuries of fiercely passionate Magyar pride went out the window, and we had him in his studio chair within two minutes.

Toward the end of the interview, I got my one-minute signal, and after thanking the guest for a most enlightening dissertation on the art of fencing, suggested that perhaps he'd be good enough to give our viewing audience a demonstration of the various techniques and nuances of the art which he had just been explaining. Through clenched teeth he muttered petulantly that he would be delighted, and after handing me one of his epees, leaped like a gazelle out of his chair and into a most graceful fencing stance. I decided that my best defence would be to keep my epee slashing back and forth in front of me like a high speed windshield wiper, and this I proceeded to do. Actually, I had the blade moving so fast back and forth that the blur of afterimages seemed like a metallic shield in front of me which I felt sure even tooth decay couldn't penetrate.

The first intimation I had that my oafish strategy wasn't working was when I looked down and noticed an ever-widening crimson stain spreading through the whiteness of my shirt just below my heart. At the time I was convinced he'd reamed out my aorta, but in true Errol Flynn tradition, I resolved to wait until the credit lines had finished rolling and the CBC cue had flashed on the screen before dying. It was a bit embarrassing when we were off the air, and a dozen big, strapping, hard-bitten stage hands came rushing over to offer their services as seconds, to learn that it was a very superficial flesh wound. Moreover, it healed so rapidly that I was only able to enjoy for about a week the satisfaction of opening my shirt in darkened corners of the CBC TV building and proudly displaying my tiny Heidelberg duelling scar below my left teat to those male members of CBC staff of whom I felt reasonably sure.

My memories of those four years of wild interviews on *Gazette* have equipped me with some wonderful opening gambits or ice-breakers, which I still use and find most effective among the sophisticated and difficult-to-impress set of the

Toronto cocktail milieu. One of my favourite throwaways is, "I'll never forget the evening Clement Atlee bit me!" While the eyebrows are still up under the hairline and the martini olive still teetering on the brink of the open mouth, it's best, if at all possible, to saunter off and become lost among the other guests before you can be pressed for details. At the risk of never again being able to use the line, I must divulge that the incident took place one evening in the *Gazette* studio when we had as guests three crew-members of a British submarine which was paying a courtesy call to Halifax. The lads brought in with them to the studio the sub's mascot — a dreadful, bad-tempered little spider monkey which, all through the interview, sat perched on my shoulder intently browsing through my hair.

I've always felt as confident about my personal hygiene as the next person, but whenever the camera dollied in for a close-up of the monkey, I could see on the studio monitor just off to one side that the little wretch was doing his best to give the impression that he was finding things — bringing the tiny pink fingers up to his beady eyes for close examination and then plunging them into my hair again for more imaginary goodies. To end the mounting and disconcerting embarrassment, I reached up in the middle of a question I was directing at the submariners and surreptitiously attempted to lift the monkey down onto my lap. Suddenly, I felt my index finger being encircled by his rotten little yellow teeth just over the knuckle and a slow, steadily increasing pressure being applied.

At the moment, one of the guests was explaining the difficulties of rescuing the doomed crews of submarines which fail to surface, and though I was beginning to feel nauseated from the pain, I felt it would be an inopportune moment to suddenly leap up and scream, "Aaaaahhhh!" all over the studio. I was able to take it for about another minute and then, convinced that my knuckle was going to crack in two, I very quietly and very formally interrupted the discussion of mass death beneath the waters by saying, "I'm awfully sorry, but if you don't get your monkey's teeth out of my shattered knuckle immediately, I'm afraid I'm going to be sick right here."

To his credit, the sailor jumped up instantly, in spite of the stunned look the non sequitur had occasioned, and made a grab for the monkey. The latter was so startled that it released my finger and leaped from my shoulder onto the camera. From there it jumped over onto the long boom from which the microphone was hanging and then over onto the curtains. The cameras then swung onto the monkey, and for the balance of the program the interview was forgotten as viewers were treated to ten minutes of the wildest acrobatics this side of the old Tarzan movies.

As it was now obvious that the monkey had completely taken over the show, I thought it might be nice to at least identify him for the viewers and so asked the submariners what his name was. At first they pretended they didn't hear me, and when I asked again, one of them, looking quite flustered, said, "We'd rower not sigh, sir." It wasn't until we were off the air that I was able to corner them and ask why on earth they were making such a production out of not divulging the monkey's name on the air. "Well, sir," was the answer, "we didn't fink it would be quite proper. We calls eem ... Clement Atlee!"

On one of my recent trips to Halifax, the CBC dug out of its TV film archives an interview on film which I'd almost forgotten. It was the one and only occasion when I was left absolutely speechless on *Gazette*. Always, no matter what went wrong, no matter what strange things the guests would come out with, no matter what havoc was wrought by animals, I would have recovered sufficiently by the end of the program to at least sign the program off in proper CBC fashion. This particular interview had taken place on the Common, a large, open stretch of grass in the city of Halifax where the Bill Lynch Travelling Show always set up shop when it was passing through. My task was to interview one of the carnival sideshow ladies named Consuela, who had an animal act.

Striving for a mood of relaxed informality, the producer had arranged Consuela and myself outstretched on the grass with her pet chimpanzee sitting between us. For fifteen minutes, Consuela answered all my questions concerning the animals in her life. She was very gypsy-looking and built like a brick cathedral. For the interview, she was wearing a brief, two-piece outfit, and during her long answers to my questions, I didn't quite know where to look. There was something morbidly fascinating about the way her bare midriff spilled down over her matador pants like a flesh-coloured truck tire. When I got my signal to wind up the interview I fell back on the old stock closing cliché, "This has been very interesting, Consuela, and now in closing could you tell us something of your future plans?"

At this point the camera began dollying in for a close-up of her, and just as they had her nicely crammed into the full frame she looked the lens straight in the eye and said, "Well, Mr. Ferguson, you might be interested to know that I'm expecting a baby elephant in nine months."

Since Halifax was a port city and very much navy-oriented, it was natural for us to decide one evening that we'd do a program on the subject of tattooing. I had been sent off the previous day to line up a tattoo artist who had set up his premises, with spider-like ingenuity, down near the waterfront, just about two pubs away from HMCS Stadacona. Sitting with me in his little back room, he told me of the brisk business he did on naval paydays. With money in their pockets and two pubs to pass before they reached his tattoo parlour, a lot of ratings would stagger in and ask to have some large-busted mermaid inked into their fore-arm. He would make one fee out of this and then, invariably, a second fee a couple of days later when the same customer would return very sober and ask to have the mermaid converted into a rose, with the tender inscription "Mother". As we sat talking and I outlined generally what we would like him to do for us in the way of a television interview, I glanced around the little room and noticed that the walls were covered with panels of beaver-board, and that each panel was crammed with an infinite variety of tattoo designs, almost all of them dealing with either Mom, Dad, Sweetheart, or God. They were all his own creations, he told me, and by the time I'd examined them all and offered him a pleasant compliment on each one, I'd won his confidence and friendship for life.

"If you think they're something," he shouted gleefully, "wait till you see this!" He then raced to the walls, rubbing his hands like a character out of Dickens, and proceeded to lift off all the beaver-board panels. Underneath the panels and lining all four walls was a monumental compilation of glossy photos, none of which seemed to have even a remote connection with Mom, Dad, Sweetheart, or God. Terrified of being run in as a found-in before being able to complete my mission, I quickly arranged an assignation with him at our TV studios for the following day and beat a hasty retreat out into the fresh air of Hollis Street.

The next evening my little Marquis de Sade turned up at the studios and gave the viewers a dandy lecture on the history and techniques of tattooing. With about five minutes of program time left, he looked up from his array of needles, inks, and designs laid out on the studio table and asked would I like a demonstration. I told him I thought that was a capital idea and looked out expectantly at the dozen or more staging and technical crew standing with their big, brawny, virgin arms folded across their chests. When I asked for a volunteer, however, there was a great shaking of heads and sotto voce chorus of, "What the Hell!"

My stomach sank when I heard my smart alec guest saying "How about you, Max? You're not afraid of a little needle are you?"

Behind my sick TV smile of false bravado, I was furious with him for putting me on the spot before thousands of Maritime viewers, and for a fleeting moment I toyed with the reprisal of telling all of them exactly what was behind all those beaver-board panels. I meekly extended a trembling white arm and stipulated that I wanted nothing more elaborate than just my two initials. Apart from a burning sensation, it was really quite painless and certainly nothing compared to Clement Atlee's teeth. As the Marquis traced out my initials, he kept up a running commentary on how the needle was penetrating at a speed of sixty times a second, how the ink was being imbedded under seven layers of skin, and how, consequently, I would carry this tattoo for life. The whole process took about thirty seconds, including the time he spent swabbing up the tiny globules of blood which oozed out along the needle's path.

After the program, while he was waiting in the TV lobby for his taxi, he thanked me profusely for the opportunity of coming on the program, and the last thing he said to me was, "You'll never know what this kind of publicity will do for me!" Obviously, neither did he. Within a couple of months, he was behind bars at Dorchester Penitentiary doing seven years for trafficking in pornographic pictures.

For the next few days my arm throbbed and took on an angry red colouring from wrist to elbow. This, however, didn't bother me half as much as the letter I received from a Surgeon-Commander in the R.C.N. in which he suggested I might like to read the paper he had just completed for the Canadian Navy showing the significant correlation between tattooing and venereal disease. I read it and hadn't felt so depressed since *Uncle Tom's Cabin*. However, within a week the arm was back to normal, and I was allowed to use the CBC bathroom facilities once again.

For sheer pandemonium, it was a guest with the mild and academic name of Professor Cato who gave me my worst moment on *Gazette*. When I had first heard the name, I envisioned a relaxed evening before the cameras, with some distinguished old Mr. Chips perhaps expounding on the use of the caesural pause in seventeenth-century French verse. However, I was soon to discover that there wasn't much of the academic about this Professor Cato. He was a 300-pound, seven-foot, professional wrestler from Japan, with one of the meanest faces you could ever hope to see. Though the war in the Pacific had been over for at least ten years I had the uneasy feeling that some blabbermouth had just told him the outcome. He wasn't the most talkative guest in the world, either, and after hearing all he had to say about his life story, his travels, his family, modern Japan, and his impressions of Canada, I realized only five minutes had been used up. In desperation I asked him if, like most professional wrestlers, he had a favourite wrestling hold. It turned out he had.

It was called the Sleeper, and furthermore, he'd be willing to demonstrate it.

Having just become a father for the fourth time, I again looked out appealingly for volunteers among the dozens of strapping bodies lounging about the studio out of camera range. Again my invitation to instant stardom was greeted with most ungrateful and sullen mutterings of, "Are you kiddin'?", "In a pig's eye!", and various other forms of negation from the darkened depths of the studio.

Faced with the choice of filling with music for the rest of the interview or submitting to the experiment myself, I took the latter course, and within thirty seconds found myself standing in a judo costume with the giant immediately behind me. After hooking a monstrous arm around my neck from behind, he explained that the Sleeper Hold was really quite painless, and that I would feel no sensation at all before dropping off into the Land of Nod. The next thing I knew the arm had tightened like a python around my neck and I was fighting for breath. My head was throbbing, my lungs were burning, and I was sure my eyeballs were going to burst. It was without a doubt the most nightmarish sensation I've ever experienced. I can remember reaching up with both hands to try to pull the arm away from my neck, and my last conscious thought was that this was a psychopathic killer and, like a fool, I'd played right into his hands.

The next thing I remember seeing was a darkened studio with a blurred red light which I knew was the camera light. I was lying on the studio floor and I could hear the far-off murmur of voices. I remembered clearly what had happened, but I couldn't understand why they had left me lying there for two weeks. I was convinced at least two weeks had passed since I'd reached up to try and break that grip. Suddenly, light seemed to come flooding into the studio, and I saw Professor Cato standing over me. I realized then that I'd only been out for a minute or so, and apart from an attack of persistent coughing, I felt perfectly alright.

I thanked Professor Cato for strangling me and had just signed the program off when the control-room door flew open, and out rushed our producer, Bill Langstroth. Not the fun-loving, happy-go-lucky Bill Langstroth we currently see leading the Jubilee Singers, but a flushed and furious Bill Langstroth, who marched up to Professor Cato like the brave little tailor and ordered him out of the studio with the admonition that he was never to show his rotten face around those parts again. I was frankly embarrassed, and after the leviathan had skulked out I asked Bill why he had been so harsh on him. It was only then that I got the full story of what had happened.

After I had dropped to the floor, I immediately went into a convulsive spasm, and Maritime viewers, including my horrified wife and children watching at home, were treated to the fine, wholesome, dinnertime family fun of sitting through a series of my spasmodic twists and jerks, with my eyeballs rolled back into my head. Panic had set in immediately in the control room, and they punched up the *Gazette* title slide while filling in the background with neutral music — probably that grand old standby in moments of doom, Handel's *Largo*. My wife had tried to phone the studio to see what had happened, but the switchboard was jammed, and she had to content herself with rummaging through old insurance policies to see which were still in force.

It would be both an inaccuracy and an exaggeration to try to give the impression from all this that *Gazette* was unremittingly a program cut from the cloth of the old Laurel and Hardy comedies. There were many evenings when nothing at all went wrong, when all of us went about our jobs with quiet efficiency and brought off the program exactly the way the producer had originally intended. The Christmas Eve edition of *Gazette* in 1957 comes to mind in this category. Our producer had decided on that evening to forego our usual format and dispense with interviews. Instead, in an attempt to recreate for the viewers a nostalgic remembrance of an old fashioned Christmas, he had grouped the three of us — Weatherman Rube Hornstein, Announcer Don Tremaine, and myself — around an open fireplace. There was to be, of course, a tinsel-draped tree, and toward the end of the half hour old Santa would appear with a real plum pudding, blazing merrily, which he would serve to us.

We were then to invite old Santa to join us in the singing of *God Rest Ye,* and somewhere in the middle of this the program would fade out. It was the type of warm, relaxed program that needed practically no rehearsing. I think we spent a maximum of five minutes mapping out camera shots and making sure that the brandy on the plum pudding would light and keep burning while Santa carried it in.

During the hour dinner break before the actual show, I drove home in bubbling good humour, had a quick bite to eat, and started to head back down to the studios. As I walked across the lawn to the driveway I noticed my English bulldog, Toughy, sitting in the snow, shivering and looking like a forlorn and miserable Quasimodo. The poor, old grotesque head, creased and wrinkled and hanging in folds, was tilted up toward me with the two big fangs almost impaling the nostrils and the two pig-like, bloodshot eyes fixing me with the most appealing look. He may have the ugliest face in dogdom, but the bulldog is quite an actor. I was able to withstand only ten seconds of this Poor Little Match Girl routine before I opened the car door and invited him in.

When my producer met me walking in through the studio door with Toughy waddling behind me, he was a bit appalled. It was common knowledge around the studios that Toughy, ever since suffering a skull fracture, had become a bit queer in the head and was known as something of a troublemaker in the neighbourhood where I lived. Quite naturally, my producer's plans for rekindling in the minds of viewers some of the beauty and poignancy of Christmas that evening had not included the lumpish hulk of a mentally deranged and physically grotesque bulldog stretched out on the studio floor at my feet. To assuage his fears, I offered to push Toughy well under the chesterfield where, I assured him, the brute would not offend any sensitive eye and would sleep peacefully through earthquake, fire, or tidal wave.

And that's the way the program began — the cosy warmth of a grate-fire reflecting off the tinsel-drenched tree, the three of us relaxed on the chesterfield and through the haze of cigar smoke allowing "fond memory to bring the light of other days around us". As in most programs which are going well, the minutes raced by, and the sudden, bellowing "Oh, ho, ho!" of Santa, waiting in the wings with the plum pudding, came as a startling reminder that we were into the last minute. That same "Oh, ho, ho!" unfortunately penetrated the bedrock of Toughy's skull and impinged rudely on the pleasurable chimera of toads, slimy mud, and whatever other delights fill a bulldog's dreams on Christmas Eve.

Only after hearing the first explosive snort did I realize,

Max and Toughy

too late, that the one thing Toughy couldn't tolerate in this world was a uniform of any kind. Out from under the chesterfield he came, in an obscene spread-eagle position because of the low clearance, but then after clawing madly to get traction he hurled himself at poor petrified Santa and engulfed at least two-thirds of the lovable old fellow's left buttock with his powerful jaws. Santa emitted a most heartrending screech of pain and threw the plum pudding, still blazing merrily, into the Christmas tree, which in turn quickly went up in flames. With the tree blazing, Toughy still hanging suspended by his teeth from Santa's buttock, and the terrified face of Santa bequeathing a legacy of traumatic scars to thousands of Maritime children, none of us had the heart to sing "God Rest Ye" as planned and, instead, merely sat there, idiotically waving like stunned robots while the credit lines rolled down inexorably over Santa's agony, and the screen went mercifully at last to black.

IX

WITHIN THREE MONTHS of that ill-fated Christmas Eve telecast, somewhere in the early spring of 1958, I received from the CBC in Toronto an invitation to move back and join the interview hosts on the popular evening program, *Tabloid*, later to change its name to *701*. There were several factors which influenced my decision to accept. First and foremost, spring was in the air, and I'm always as prone as the next fellow to the giddy and restive spell nature seems to cast over all of us at such a time, Then, too, Toughy's misdemeanours around the neighbourhood were beginning to catch up with him. In fact, at that very time, there was a steadily mounting hue and cry to have the poor misshapen social misfit despatched to the Great Kennel in the Sky, and I felt that a move to Toronto would perhaps enable him to build a new life under an assumed name. This, as fate was later to decree, was not to be the case. Three weeks after we arrived in Toronto, in one of his misguided and over-zealous attempts to protect the children, he bit Punch Imlach's daughter and was finally given, as they would say in hockey circles, a major.

Since I was no longer to have the Atlantic Ocean on my doorstep, I determined to settle as close to water as I could when we arrived in Toronto in the late summer of 1958. By paying only $12,000 more than I had paid for my fifteen room home outside Halifax, I was able to pick up a charming little bird-house whose total floor space would just nicely fit into my old forty-five foot living room in Halifax. However, it was perched on the Scarborough Bluffs, just a handy two-minute walk from that great natural asset with which Toronto is blessed, Lake Ontario. Swimming, of course, was out of the question due to the immense tonnage of sewage and industrial waste which has been, is, and will continue to be poured into what otherwise might be a summer paradise for hundreds of

140

AND NOW ... HERE'S MAX

thousands of sticky, panting summer inmates of that fast-growing and progressive city. However, it was still a lovely place to walk, along the sand beach at the foot of the towering bluffs. My nostalgia for the East Coast was still powerfully acute, but I soon discovered that by walking along the Lake Ontario strand mentally reciting the opening lines of *Harmony Harbour* — "We give you ships and tides and men" — I could create a rather pleasurable substitute, especially since my shoes, oozing down the ever-present mire of putrefying and semi-decomposed fish, would emit a squooshing sound somewhat akin to turgid and obscene surf breaking in tiny waves on some far-off rotten shore.

Since we were one of the first families to move into this little Shangri-la, there were very few neighbours on our street. One of the first I met was a distraught housewife about four doors down who had phoned to borrow some saucepans. When I discovered she was Mrs. Punch Imlach, I assumed Punch was unexpectedly arriving home with the entire Leaf team for dinner. It turned out, however, that the rain was pouring through a dozen or more leaks in her roof, and her kitchen arsenal could only cope with part of the deluge. While I helped her make as aesthetic an arrangement as possible of the various pots and pans around her living room, she recounted the narrow escape she'd had the day before while attempting to close the garage door. It was the type of sliding garage door that you start with a pull and which then continues under its own momentum with an outward and downward movement. However, when she gave it its initial pull, this one kept right on going straight out, cleared her head by about two inches and landed with a crash halfway down the driveway.

I suppose every neighbourhood has its "darling couple", and we certainly had ours. They were just around the corner from us — very young, most attractive, and full of friendly smiles when you waved hello. But there seemed to be a certain reticence and shyness about them. They were a familiar sight in the early evening after dinner — she, sitting on the front steps, looking like a small girl as she pushed the

141

baby-buggy back and forth, while he, always just a few feet away, worked in the front flower bed, trowelling and planting to make the little bungalow pretty for her. With their baby, a Siamese cat, and a little pet monkey, this winsome couple created a real dilemma among the dozen or so couples who were already living in the area. Everyone wanted so much to mother them and yet feared to intrude into what was so obviously a honeymoon environment.

One evening my small son came back after visiting the couple to see their monkey. He told us that the nice lady had said he couldn't see the monkey, because it had turned into a gorilla overnight and was loose in the neighbourhood. I was still pondering this strange Charles Addams' twist to our little Shirley Temple 'round the corner when, two days later, the Toronto papers hit the streets with blazing headlines: POLICE SMASH LARGEST VICE RING EVER. Sometime during the night, Toronto's finest had kicked in the front door of the little love nest, pumped tear-gas all through it, and overpowered Canada's Sweetheart as she came at them with a loaded gun. After discovering dozens of phones and a list of clients as thick as the Toronto phone book, they announced it had been the largest

Tabloid, 1958
(l.-r.) Percy Saltzman, Max, Ted Pope, Joyce Davidson, John O'Leary

call-girl operation in the history of Toronto. After that, the only excitement in the neighbourhood was when we were awakened now and again at about three in the morning to see our neighbour two doors away handcuffed to a police cruiser and singing at the top of his voice with drunken nostalgia all the old rousers from his Afrika Korps days with Rommel. But I never did find out what his trouble was.

My interview work as a co-host on *Tabloid* began that fall. After four years of the leisurely, unrehearsed, and unscripted approach of *Gazette,* it took some getting used to *Tabloid's* format — and I'm afraid I never really did. *Tabloid* was heavily scripted and had a predilection for the jiffy capsule-type interview. A staccato-like pace was essential. This, of course, was often a blessing when you were handed a vapid young Hollywood starlet whose entire mental reservoir would be depleted in less than a minute. It could, conversely, be terribly frustrating when your guest was an interesting one with something to say.

One evening, for example, I was informed that my guest was to be a bright and alert editor from a large Tokyo newspaper. He was in Canada attending the Couchiching Conference. Since the theme of the Conference that year was "Changing Asia", the *Tabloid* producer took me aside and suggested I tackle the interview from this angle, probing my guest for his views on the historic, social, political, and economic changes taking place in modern-day Japan. "Right!" I shouted with mounting enthusiasm for one of the first real challenges I'd encountered up to that time on the program. "How much time have I got?".

There was a moment of brow furrowing and bottom-lip biting — " I think I can give you pretty close to three minutes."

My fondest and certainly most vivid memory of *Tabloid* was the night they sent me down to the gala opening of *Camelot* at the O'Keefe Centre dressed as one of my Rawhide characters, Elizabeth Barrett Blueing. The TV make-up girls spent about an hour converting me into Miss Blueing, attaching long artificial eyelashes, executing a most voluptuous rosebud mouth, applying rouge and eyeliner, and topping off the whole effect with a very convincing wig. Then I was handed over to the costume people, who draped me in a gorgeously dowdy and decadent turn-of-the-century gown, with yards of chiffon boa wrapped around my neck. With a pair of ornate earrings dangling from my lobes and white evening gloves up to my elbows, I was led out the front door of the TV building on Jarvis Street. Waiting for me in the parking lot was a gigantic 1924 Packard open touring car, with a uniformed and gauntleted chauffeur mounted high up on the driver's seat. It was a bitterly cold late fall evening, and I had to clamp my teeth down hard on my long cigarette holder in order to keep them from chattering. I was seated with haughty regality on the back seat about eight feet off the ground, and we rolled magnificently off the parking lot and into the Jarvis Street traffic on our way to the biggest and most talked about theatrical evening in Toronto's history.

As one heads south on Jarvis Street, it gets progressively rougher and tougher. A few years ago it used to be rough and tough all the way down. Those were the days when the CBC was frequently used as a forward observation post for Toronto morality squads from which they could peer out the CBC windows through binoculars on a vast empire of sin in all directions. In those days the CBC was known as the only non-profit endeavour on Jarvis Street. However, the CBC today sits just on the southern extremity of the respectable and salvaged northern end of the street.

We had progressed in our stately Packard about four blocks south on Jarvis and were approaching the intersection of Jarvis and Richmond just as the lights turned red. As I sat looking out from my lofty perch like the Queen Mother doing a tour of the London slums, I noticed a drunk teetering back and forth on the curb and attempting to bring into clearer focus the incongruous apparition of opulence which had just invaded his particular corner of Rubbydubland. You could see the worn and haggard face slowly twisting into a sneer as great waves of scorn and resentment welled up at the sight of all this flagrantly ostentatious wealth parked in front of him. Suddenly, he half fell, half lurched off the curb and began weaving his way out into Jarvis Street so that he ended up right beside the Packard. There was all the fury of the French Revolution distilled into that one bloodshot glare as he hissed drunkenly, "I shupposhe you thlink you're really shumbodly!"

From high atop my perch I fluttered my one-inch eyelashes and flashed him a warm noblesse oblige smile of understanding. Then leaning out over the side of the car and addressing him as "my good fellow", I indicated in one concise, imperious command that I would like him to go away. The two words I employed were straight out of his own earthy vocabulary, but when spoken in the plummy, stage English of Miss Blueing the effect was particularly stunning. With the mouth hanging open in slack stupefaction he weaved backwards to the curb, over the same erratic route, like a film sequence run in reverse.

As we neared the O'Keefe Centre, which faces onto Front Street, I could see a long cortege of chauffeur-driven private limousines moving at something less than Royal Tour speed along Front Street and disgorging at the main entrance Toronto's "beauty and its chivalry". Our old Packard was approaching Front Street at a right angle from the north, and it was necessary to make a left turn onto Front and worm our way into the cortege. After waiting a few minutes without any space opening up between the limousines, we bullied our way in between the front and rear bumpers of two magnificent old vintage machines, and I held one arm aloft in a genteel version of a traffic cop's signal to stop. Standing up with my boa and light summer dress flapping in the breeze I bellowed at the long line of suddenly arrested limousines in Miss Blueing's English contralto, "Stop, I say! Stop, the lot of you! Have you forgotten common good manners? Make room for us this instant! Such a pushy, ill-bred pack!" At this instant, the back windows of about ten limousines within range of my tongue-lashing all rolled down simultaneously and out popped the startled heads of Toronto's finest old families — magnificent old dowager empresses all primped and preened as if they were out to take in the premiere of *Chu Chin Chow*. The incredible thing was that every one of them looked like me made up as Elizabeth Barrett

Blueing.

Our old open Packard was now in line with the best of them and inching its way along the front of the O'Keefe, where an honour guard of R.M.C. cadets from Kingston stood rigidly at attention. I blew them all kisses and told them they were dear boys to turn out on such a cold night. There were one or two titters in the back row, but the front rank looked bewildered and terrified. Suddenly, a liveried doorman appeared and in finest Uriah Heep fashion, with bowed head, opened the rear door of the Packard for me and I alighted. The press, particularly fashion reporters, were milling all about the entrance, and as I moved graciously into the O'Keefe lobby one or two ran after me and with great politeness asked me my name. I replied haughtily, "Elizabeth Barrett Blueing."

Then they asked the standard question which I had heard them asking the legitimate matriarchs who had just preceded me, "Could you please tell us something about the dress you're wearing?" I suddenly realized that in spite of my outlandish get-up, these reporters and indeed all the people standing around staring curiously but with obvious respect, were accepting me as a bona fide, if eccentric, member of Toronto's top social stratum.

"This dress," I replied, "has been in my family for over one hundred years." I had intended to stop there, but when I saw the reporter furiously scribbling, I couldn't resist adding, "In fact, my grandmother was buried in it." He was still writing that one down as I swept off grandly and was engulfed by the crowds inside the foyer.

The original plan as devised by my producer (the arrival was being filmed for later use on *Tabloid)* was for me to make an entrance and walk down the long O'Keefe aisle to a seat which had been reserved for me right beside the Lieutenant-Governor. I felt this would be overdoing things, so I headed for one of the side doors, where my driver had arranged to meet me with the Packard. Perched once again on the back seat, we drove around to the front of the O'Keefe again where the endless stream of first-night fashion plates was still flowing in. A lot of them were staring at me as we drove past in the opposite direction. They were obviously puzzled that this old belle dame should be leaving when it was still about twenty minutes to curtain time. I think I managed to contribute to their confusion by announcing in loud tones as I passed them, "A most over-rated production ... it's certainly going to need lengthening." With that, we swept away into the night, back to the CBC, mission accomplished.

X

W HY DID YOU ever drop Rawhide?" This is a constantly recurring question in my radio mail and is still the
most frequently asked question among people I meet socially
in my wanderings outside the CBC walls. Though I always try
to express it euphemistically, the simple answer is that I was
sick and tired of him. After seventeen continuous years of performing as Rawhide on CBC radio, it began to dawn on me
with horror that this could go on and on over the years until I
would no longer be faking the old fellow's voice — it would
probably be my own natural speaking voice. Thus in 1961,
when the CBC relieved me of the hopeless task of trying
to compete with early evening television and offered me a
new half-hour spot in the early morning, I not only jumped
at the opportunity but decided to make a completely clean
sweep and change the entire format of the Rawhide program.
I was looking for some kind of format which would keep me
alert and interested by restoring some of the lost challenge
and excitement of the early days of the Rawhide show. And
so I set myself the task of bringing in the morning paper two
hours before broadcast time each morning and trying to come
up with two skits based on news stories which had just appeared. The idea had excitement and challenge alright — it
was like a radio version of Russian roulette, except that the
nervous exhilaration came not in trying to avoid the *loaded*
chamber but the empty one, that awful morning when the creative process won't function at all and I must go on the air
with nothing. Though the horror of such a situation has often
been the subject matter of my dreams and has many a time
wrenched me rudely awake in the middle of the night, in real
life I've managed for the past five years to meet the relentless
deadline.

In the late summer of 1961 the CBC, functioning like the

mechanism of a fine Swiss watch, began making preparations for my new morning series to start on Labour Day morning at exactly 7:35 a.m. E.D.T. A host of details were attended to; network time had to be cleared at that hour, studio facilities booked, producer assigned, engineer and sound-effects man requisitioned, newsmen in the various regions alerted to glean their local papers for stories and telex them in during the night so that I'd have them in the morning, talent in all the regions auditioned and selected to contribute to the musical portion of the program each morning. Nothing was overlooked.

When I arrived at 5:00 a.m. that first morning, bright-eyed and bushy-tailed, I discovered the CBC had overlooked only one tiny detail. The premises at 354 Jarvis Street were locked tight and I couldn't get in. This strange practice by old Mother CBC of bolting up tight after donning her nightcap and putting out the milk bottles is obviously a throw-back to the days when the old red-brick hovel was a private finishing school for young ladies. Then such precautions were essential, in view of the questionable neighbourhood, if the young charges were to bring their maidenhead to marriage. But the Havergal girls have long since gone, and the current night-cleaning staff of the CBC is not only all male but quite sexually unattractive to boot, so there's no damn excuse.

After wasting a precious half hour of time pounding, kicking, and yelling at all three doors, front, back, and side, I wandered into the little CBC courtyard that lies just under the windows of the announcers' lounge. I could see the silhouette of the CBC early morning man, De B. Holly, moving about inside, so I threw up a few tiny pebbles that hit the window and caught his attention. He opened the window, and I was able to climb the fire escape, throw a leg in over the sill, and gain entry. After the first week or two of gaining access in this fashion, I had depleted the courtyard of pebbles and so adopted the practice of simply yelling up at De B.'s peripatetic silhouette, "Rapunzel! Rapunzel! Let down your long hair!"

This ritual lasted only until the inevitable morning a week or so later when my arrival in the announcers' lounge was followed moments later by a loud, metallic clanging of footsteps racing up the fire escape. In over the window sill came the uniformed leg of a security guard, followed by a flushed and wide-eyed face demanding to know who I was, what I was doing there, and how long I'd known Rapunzel. There was something awfully ludicrous about standing there at five in the morning recounting a child's fairy tale to a man old enough to be my father while his hand rested nervously throughout on his side-arm.

In fact, as I reach this stage in my rambling yarn, I'm forced to admit that there's been something awfully ludicrous about the entire twenty years that have elapsed since I first stepped through the looking-glass into Canadian radio. To those who have followed me this far still hoping, perhaps, for at least a few crumbs of serious thought on the subject of national radio in this country — my apologies. Such a task I leave to Messrs. Gordon, Fowler, and a long list of others who will undoubtedly follow. As Rawhide I once described the CBC as a big, fat, motherly white leghorn, with one scaly foot planted in Newfoundland and the other in B.C., so that the intervening space was kept warm and protected by the soft, downy underbelly, allowing her little chicks to scamper about, peeping and cheeping to their hearts' content.

As Max Ferguson I can't offer a much better analogy. I see the CBC as a sort of domestic British Empire. Both were created and developed by a rather insular breed, exhibiting alternate flashes of brilliance and idiocy. At this moment there are many critics who would extend the analogy even further, gloomily predicting that the sun is already setting on the CBC also, and that, beset from without and within, its complete disintegration is close at hand. Certainly, to all those who help guide the CBC ship of state, the prospect of turbulent and dangerous waters ahead must occasion moments of doubt, confusion, and uncertainty. To all these men I bequeath this final anecdote — or, if you will, parable — from which I hope they may gain some small measure of assurance and inner strength.

Some years ago, when the CBC was young and before its elders led the flock to the present temple beside the quiet-flowing traffic of Jarvis Street, the fountainhead of radio enlightenment in this country was in a building on Davenport Road in Toronto. Working in the building at the time was an executive who had a bit of a problem. Though we all have our Achilles heels, the frequency with which this individual was picked up by Toronto's finest for operating while under the influence would seem to suggest that his was more of an Achilles foot. He was eventually informed, in no uncertain terms by an irate magistrate, that if such an offence should occur once more, he would be almost certain to lose his car, licence, and freedom to come and go. With the terrible admonition still ringing in his ears, he left a CBC office get-together one evening just at rush-hour and barrelled his car with great abandon down the long driveway beside the CBC building, out into the traffic of Davenport Road, where he crashed broadside into a perfectly innocent motorist. Even through the foggy fumes of his recently consumed office lunch the full enormity of what he'd done hit him like a sledgehammer. Sick with the pangs of self-recrimination, he could only sit and stare in quiet desperation at the damage he had done. Then as he stared, the twisted door of the other car slowly opened, and a body slithered out onto the road. Rising to its knees, it began hobbling toward him in this position across Davenport Road, like Toulouse Lautrec, calling to him in a very thick, slurred, and drunken voice, "Don't call the police! I'll pay for everything! It's all my fault! Just don't call the police! Don't report it!"

Sail on, O CBC — sail on! Should dark hours lie ahead for *you,* may Fortune smile with similar sweetness.

APPENDIX

SIXTY YEARS HAVE passed since some of the events related in this memoir. Though many of the characters of whom Max writes need no further introduction, others, to younger readers at least, are no longer household names. These brief biographical sketches will, the editors hope, give some context to both categories of people mentioned.

Joel Aldred: Radio and later television announcer and businessman.

Andrew Allan: National head of CBC Radio Drama, 1943-1955; later the Shaw Festival's first artistic director.

Ted Allan: Author of *Lies My Father Told Me*; pseudonym of Alan Herman.

Clement Atlee: British Prime Minister, 1945-1951.

James Bannerman: Radio announcer and television host. "James Bannerman" was a professional pseudonym; his real name was John McNaught.

Marilyn Bell: At the age of 16, in September 1964, became the first person to swim Lake Ontario.

Harry J. Boyle: Author of a number of books, two of which won the Leacock Medal (1964 & 1976). CBC broadcaster and in the sixties and seventies, vice-chairman and chairman of the CRTC.

Earl Cameron: CBC radio newsreader (who presented news of the D-Day landings); first anchorman on what became *The*

National.

Peter Dawson: Australian bass-baritone singer.

Jack Dempsey: American heavyweight boxer.

Madame de Sevigny: The Marquise de Sévigné (1626-1696) was a prominent figure in the literary salons of seventeenth-century Paris and the author of a large collection of letters published shortly after her death.

John Drainie: Radio and film actor, as well as host on the controversial and short-lived but influential television newsmagazine *This Hour Has Seven Days.*

Elwood Glover: Announcer and host of radio and eventually television programmes; he worked for the CBC from 1938 into the seventies.

Lorne Greene: Born Lyon Green, he was a radio announcer with the CBC beginning in 1939; he was referred to as both "the Voice of Canada" and "the Voice of Doom", the latter for his reading of the war headlines and casualty figures. He went on to star in the television western *Bonanza* and the original *Battlestar Galactica*, and to host the nature show *Lorne Greene's New Wilderness.*

Rube Hornstein: Physicist, meteorologist, officer in charge of Eastern Air Command's meteorological section throughout most of the Second World War, and author; he provided weather announcing for CBC radio and on the television show *Gazette* while in charge of the Halifax Atlantic Weather Centre.

Punch Imlach: NHL coach and general manager of the Toronto Maple Leafs from 1958 to 1969 and briefly, in the early eighties.

Skookum Jim: Skookum Jim Mason is credited with the gold discovery in Bonanza Creek in the Yukon that began the Klondike Gold Rush.

Jubilee Singers: *Singalong Jubilee*, one of the CBC's most popular shows of the era, was on air from 1961 to 1974. Several famous singers, including Anne Murray and Catherine McKinnon, began their careers on it.

Michael Kane: Actor in a number of American and Canadian film and television productions, as well as many National Film Board productions.

Kinsey Kids: Refers to Alfred Kinsey and the Kinsey Reports on human sexual behaviour.

Bill Langstroth: Co-host and associate producer on *Singalong Jubilee*.

Carmen Lombardo: Singer and composer.

Guy Lombardo: Bandleader of *The Royal Canadians*.

Esse W. Ljungh: CBC radio announcer from 1942; head of CBC Radio Drama 1957-1969, although he took over the duties of the position from Andrew Allan in 1955.

Victor McLaglen: British-born Canadian boxer and actor.

Ed McCurdy: Songwriter and folksinger.

Allan McFee: CBC radio announcer and host of *Allan McFee's Eclectic Circus*. For years, he introduced both *The Max Ferguson Show* and *The Royal Canadian Air Farce*. His introduction to the former was always, "And now ... here's Max."

Joe Niosi: Played bass for the radio variety show *The Happy*

Gang, 1945-1959.

"Ma Perkins": *Ma Perkins* was an American radio soap opera airing from 1939 to 1960. "Ma" was the main character.

Christopher Plummer: World-renowned Shakespearean actor; has also done extensive work in film and television.

E.P. Taylor: Extremely wealthy Canadian businessman.

Gene Tunney: Boxer who twice defeated Jack Dempsey.

Murray Westgate: Canadian actor.

Byng Whitteker: Host of the children's show *Small Types Club* on CBC Radio in the nineteen-fifties.

Austin Willis: Actor and television host.

J. Frank Willis: CBC radio announcer, noted for live reports from the Moose River Mine disaster in 1936.

Other Books from Sybertooth Inc.

BY DONALD JACK

It's Me Again: Volume III of The Bandy Papers

ISBN-13: 9780973950519

In this classic novel of the First World War, ace pilot Bartholomew Bandy struggles against his adjutant, his adjutant's pigeon, a defective parachute design, a new German bi-plane, and the Bolshevik army, managing to get promoted to general in the process...

Me Bandy, You Cissie: Volume IV of The Bandy Papers

ISBN: 9780973950571
(winner of the Leacock Medal for Humour)

The Great War may be finished, but Bartholomew Bandy isn't. After not quite succeeding in defeating communism in Russia, he returns to the New World, but what with carrying airmail and trying to start his own aviation business while dodging flappers and bootleggers, Bandy hardly has time to be a silent movie star... This edition includes the radio play "Banner's Headline".

This One's On Me: Volume VI of The Bandy Papers

ISBN: 9780973950557

It's 1924; Bandy is making a solo flight across the Atlantic in the Gander, a seaplane of his own design. Not for fame though – he's fleeing from arrest for train robbery, from his job as Minister of Defence, and from his would-be assassin and friend George Garanine.

Me So Far: Volume VII of The Bandy Papers

ISBN: 9780973950502

Bandy has finally found a secure post-war job, as commander of the Maharajah of Jhamjarh's new air force. The only problem is, the British Raj are not so happy with him for setting up a rival air power inside British India.

Hitler Versus Me: Volume VIII of the Bandy Papers

ISBN-13: 9780968802489

It's 1940, and the intrepid air ace of WWI is eager to join the fight against Germany. Unfortunately, everyone seems to think Bandy is too old to be flying Spitfires, and should go quietly into retirement to polish his medals. Bandy, however, has other ideas... (includes the novelette "Where Did Rafe Madison Go?")

Stalin Versus Me: Volume IX of The Bandy Papers

ISBN-13: 9780968802472

In the aftermath of the Normandy invasion, Bandy continues to bob through the ranks like a cork at sea.

The Canvas Barricade

ISBN-13: 9780968802496

In print for the first time, Donald Jack's comedy *The Canvas Barricade* was the first modern play performed on the main stage of the Stratford Festival (1961).

Coming soon:

Me Too: Volume V of The Bandy Papers

www.sybertooth.ca

Other Books from Sybertooth Inc.

The Captain Star Omnibus
By Steven Appleby
ISBN: 9780973950564

From the creator of the cult-classic *Captain Star* TV cartoon series: the first collection of comic strips tracing the strange but illustrious career of Captain Jim Star – the greatest hero any world has ever known.

Letters from Helen
By Helen VanWart
Edited by Douglas Lochhead

A collection of letters and photographs from a New Brunswick girl travelling to Leipzig, Germany to study music just before the outbreak of the First World War. *(forthcoming, 2010)*

Quests and Kingdoms
A Grown-Up's Guide to Children's Fantasy Literature
By K.V. Johansen
ISBN-13: 9780968802441

"... this is not only a fine reference tool but a finely-written book...This is undoubtedly a seminal work guaranteed to stimulate discussion on children's literature..." *–Books in Canada*
"What truly amazes, though, is Johansen's reliability and depth of knowledge...and her accuracy with facts...The sheer volume of knowledge on display here could earn Johansen honors for scholarship. This is a truly useful reference book..." *-Mythprint* (Bulletin of the Mythopoeic Society)
"...a lively, thoughtful read, and a useful reference volume." - *Terri Windling*

Beyond Window-Dressing? Canadian Children's Fantasy at the Millennium
By K.V. Johansen
ISBN: 9780968802458

"I applaud the honesty and forthrightness of her analyses. Far too often, reviews of children's books provide little more than vague plot summaries with very little, if any, questioning of the aesthetic or literary value of a text. Not so with Johansen's analyses. She has her opinions and she quite adroitly defends them. She establishes clear criteria for what she considers a valid and valuable fantasy, and judges each text accordingly. And, I must admit, I found her criticism of even some of Canada's literary icons both refreshing and, more significantly, quite convincing." *–Canadian Literature*

Love on the Marsh: A Long Poem
by Douglas Lochhead
ISBN: 9780973950533

This long poem in 100 stanzas is described by Lochhead as "an extension of *High Marsh Road*" and "brother and sister to it". The diary-like entries, a form to which Lochhead has frequently returned over the years, can also be compared to his work in *The Panic Field*. By turns earthy and ethereal, a pilgrimage through a landscape of grass and sky and tumultuous emotions, *Love on the Marsh* revisits the High Marsh Road with a new eye and finds in it the self-examining, self-discovering heart.

www.sybertooth.ca

LaVergne, TN USA
04 December 2009
166013LV00001B/21/P